SCIENCE ETHICS

OTHER BOOKS
BY DAVID E. NEWTON

Science and Social Issues

Nutrition for You

Understanding Venereal Disease

Chemistry Updated

Biology Updated

Sexual Health

*An Introduction to
Molecular Biology*

*Learning Facts and Attitudes
about Human Sexuality*

Sexual Questions

Knowledge for a Nuclear World

DAVID E. NEWTON

SCIENCE ETHICS

FRANKLIN WATTS / 1987
NEW YORK / LONDON / TORONTO / SYDNEY
AN IMPACT BOOK

Cartoons and photographs courtesy of: Photo Researchers, Inc.:
pp. 15 and 51 (Guy Gillette), 41 (Arthur Glauberman), 57 (Catherine
Ursillo), 64 (James Prince); ROTHCO Cartoons: pp. 18 (© Buresch),
25, 29, 53, 59, and 78 (© Punch), 34 (© Carol Simpson-Environmental Action,
Washington, D.C.), 54 (© Levine), 85 (© E.A. Harris-Canada), 107
(© Renault-The Sacramento Bee, California), 110 (Arnold Wiles);
The Bettman Archive, Inc.: pp. 22, 31, 103; WHO/Best Institute: p. 43;
The Los Angeles Times: p. 69 (Conrad); Lookout Mountain Laboratory,
USAF: p. 75; Sidney Harris: pp. 76, 83; UPI/Bettmann Newsphotos: p. 87;
Bulletin of the Atomic Scientists: p. 94 (Lisa Grayson/Art Director);
AT & T Bell Laboratories: p. 98

Library of Congress Cataloging-in-Publication Data

Bibliography: p.
Includes index.
Summary: Discusses ethical problems surrounding vivisection,
genetic engineering, and other fields of scientific research.
1. Research—Moral and ethical aspects—Juvenile literature.
2. Science—Moral and ethical aspects—Juvenile literature.
[1. Science—Moral and ethical aspects. 2. Research—Moral
and ethical aspects] I. Title.
Q180.55.M67N49 1987   174'.95   87-10490
ISBN 0-531-10419-2

Copyright © 1987 by David E. Newton
All rights reserved
Printed in the United States of America
6 5 4 3 2 1

To Everett Mendelsohn

*He never knew the seeds
he was planting.*

CONTENTS

Introductory Note
11

CHAPTER ONE
Ethics and Science
13

CHAPTER TWO
Scientific Research
27

CHAPTER THREE
Research on Animals
and Humans
49

CHAPTER FOUR
Genetic Research
62

CHAPTER FIVE
Military Research
72

CHAPTER SIX
When Scientists Speak Out
81

CHAPTER SEVEN
Science as Big Business
101

Notes
116

Bibliography
118

Periodicals and Organizations
122

Index
124

SCIENCE ETHICS

INTRODUCTORY NOTE

Each chapter in this book opens with an imaginary case study, a "dilemma." These dilemmas show some of the ways ethical questions arise in a scientist's life.

The case studies all describe fictional situations in which a scientist faces a choice among two or more courses of action. The introductory situations are not real; the people mentioned in them are not real. The situations described and the choices presented *are* typical, however, of those that many scientists face today. Real-life cases are discussed later in each chapter. Individuals mentioned in these studies are real.

1
ETHICS AND SCIENCE

DR. HENRY'S DILEMMA

Dr. Vivian Henry has worked for the Mira-Cure Pharmaceutical Company for almost two years. She felt lucky to get the job with Mira-Cure after finishing graduate school. Jobs in her field of interest have been scarce, and she was chosen over fifty other applicants.

Dr. Henry's work assignment at Mira-Cure has been with a new drug called Suppresin. Suppresin promises to be a highly effective treatment for mild pain. The company hopes that the new drug will become as popular as aspirin, Tylenol, and other pain-killers now on the market. After eight years of research, officials at Mira-Cure are ready to request governmental approval for the release of Suppresin to the general public.

Some of Dr. Henry's latest research, however, worries her. Her studies show that rats who have been fed Suppresin have a somewhat higher rate of liver cancer than do rats who have not received the drug. Dr. Henry suspects, but cannot be sure, that the higher rate of cancer is caused by Suppresin. She wonders if the drug is really ready for use by humans.

On the other hand, Dr. Harley Hanley, director of research at Mira-Cure, is not so sure about Dr. Henry's results or her conclusions. Other studies have shown no increase in cancer among animals fed Suppresin. Dr. Hanley wonders if Dr. Henry has made an error in her research. He believes that, all factors considered, the drug can really be considered safe and is ready for public sale.

Besides, the Mira-Cure Company is eager to begin selling Suppresin. Research on the drug has cost the company millions of dollars so far. The time has come, the company feels, to start earning some of that money back.

All factors considered, Dr. Hanley believes that the time has come to seek approval for Suppresin from the Food and Drug Administration (FDA). Following standard procedures, he will send all relevant research on Suppresin to the FDA when he makes his request—all except Dr. Henry's latest studies on the drug.

Dr. Henry is not sure that is the right thing to do. Should she continue to argue with her boss, Dr. Hanley? Or should she go over his head and talk to someone higher up in the company? Perhaps she should just try not to worry about her results and go along with the company's decision to request government approval for the drug.

ETHICAL ISSUES: CHOICES BETWEEN RIGHT AND WRONG

In this story, Dr. Henry has to make some choices. She can either try to stop the release of Suppresin or remain silent. The choices that Dr. Henry makes will depend on what she thinks is right or wrong for her to do in this situation.

Questions of right and wrong, of good and bad, are called ethical questions. When Dr. Henry, Dr. Hanley, and other scientists like them have to choose among various courses of action, they have to make *ethical decisions*. People in every walk of life are confronted with ethical choices all the time. You might have an opportunity to

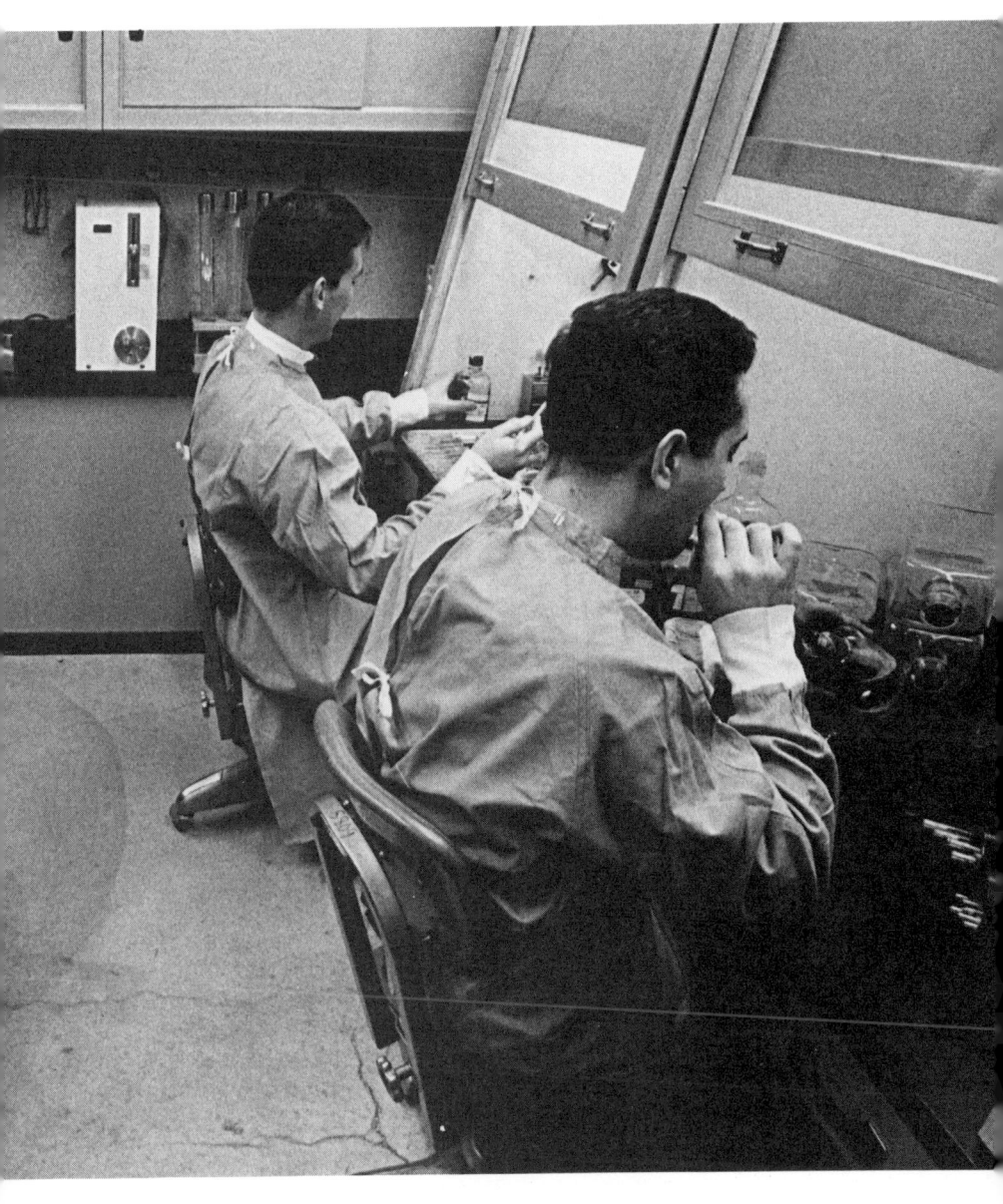

The technicians in this cancer research lab test the effects of thousands of compounds on viruses.

cheat on a math test for which you didn't study. Deciding whether or not to cheat is an ethical decision for you. When playing a game, you might want to "bend the rules" a little to give you an advantage over an opponent. Choosing whether to bend the rules or not is also an ethical choice.

Ethical questions arise in every occupation. A lawyer may have to decide, for example, if he or she should withhold evidence that might be damaging to a client. The choice may not be easy because the additional evidence might lead to the client's conviction. A doctor may have to choose between doing everything possible to keep a very old person alive and simply letting that person "slip away" and die. Is it right to keep the person alive at any cost or to let the person die?

Doctors and lawyers have formal codes of ethics. These codes of ethics describe the kinds of actions which are *right* and *wrong* in the fields of medicine and law. When a person becomes a lawyer or a doctor, he or she takes a pledge to live and work according to the code of the profession.

Ethical questions in science go back hundreds of years, to the very beginning of modern science itself. In most cases, scientists have no formal written code of ethics, like those in law and medicine. Still, some kinds of action in science *are* generally considered to be "right" or "wrong." For example, almost all scientists would agree it is *right* to give credit when a person makes a discovery and *wrong* to lie about the results of one's own research. Most ethical questions in science, however, have no simple answer.

THE COMPLEXITY OF ETHICAL ISSUES

Ethical questions are difficult because they involve so many factors. Dr. Henry has to think, first of all, about the way her decision will affect her *personal* life. If she pushes her ideas too hard or causes too much trouble for the company, she may lose her job. She will have to think also about the way her co-workers and supervisors will treat her if she continues to disagree with them.

Like all of us, Dr. Henry makes decisions based on certain *religious and moral* considerations also. Suppose she has been taught that a person fights for what she believes is right "no matter what." Then, losing her job and friends may be the price she has to pay to keep Suppresin off the market.

Moral arguments work both ways too. If Dr. Henry accepts employment at Mira-Cure, does she then owe the company a certain amount of loyalty? Is it unethical to accept a paycheck from the company and then argue with the company's decisions?

Economic factors also make a difference. Suppose Dr. Henry decides to fight against the release of Suppresin. She may feel proud and happy that she has made the right ethical decision, but she still has to eat! More than that, the Mira-Cure job is a wonderful career opportunity that may not come along again.

The company's economic welfare should be considered also. After spending a lot of time and money on the development of Suppresin, perhaps it's only fair that Mira-Cure now have a chance to make a profit on the drug.

In many cases, *legal* questions affect an ethical decision. The U.S. Congress has established certain guidelines for the release of drugs, cosmetics, and food additives to the marketplace. Mira-Cure is required by law to send all relevant test results to the FDA when it submits any drug for approval.

As this case illustrates, however, that process is not always a simple one. The company decides what research it will send to the FDA. In this instance, Dr. Hanley has decided that Dr. Henry's research is irrelevant or wrong, and he will not include it in his application. That may or may not be an ethical decision.

Also, if Dr. Henry's research is correct, the company may release a dangerous product to the marketplace. People's health may be harmed, and they may sue the company for selling a product that was not properly tested.

Finally, most societies and most social institutions have certain *ethical standards*. For example, premeditated murder is usually considered to be wrong in most societies. Societies generally do not allow individuals to argue that they have an ethical right to take someone else's life simply because that action will be to their own personal, social, economic, or emotional benefit.

In many cases, society's ethical rules—written or unwritten—can be a powerful influence on our ultimate decisions about right and wrong. We may be able to think of many personal reasons for following a particular course of action. But we may also know that friends, business colleagues, and society at large think that that choice is wrong. The force of this social pressure, then, can override any and all personal factors involved in our decision.

What decision did you come to about Dr. Henry's dilemma? Did you find yourself taking first one position, then another? That's common in trying to deal with ethical issues. We may want to do one thing for one reason, but a different thing for another reason. The decision that Dr. Henry finally makes will come about after weighing and comparing many factors, such as job, income, career opportunities, public welfare, legal restrictions, economic factors, loyalty, personal moral beliefs, and ethical standards of our society and its institutions.

THE GAME OF SCIENCE

Ethics means "playing by the rules of the game." We can learn about ethical issues in science by understanding some of the rules by which "the game of science" is played.

The *purpose* of the game of science is fairly simple: to make true statements about the natural world. These statements can be as simple as "The melting point of ice is 0°C," or as comprehensive as "all objects in the universe feel an attraction to one another."

The primary *method* by which these statements develop is observation. Some scientists observe nature directly. Astronomers, for example, learn about stars by studying them through telescopes. But most scientists study nature through experiments, specially designed situations which allow them to study one specific part of nature at a time. Scientists report the results of their observations and experiments in written reports, articles in professional journals, speeches at conventions, and informal conversation at other scientific meetings.

Probably the most important rule of the game of science tells when we know a statement is *true* in science. After all, anyone can look through a telescope or do an experiment and write down some observations. But how do we know those observations are true?

The answer is by *confirmation*. Once scientist A writes down a result, other scientists will begin to use that result in their own work. As they use the new idea, they'll find out whether or not the idea "works." If it does work time after time, the new idea is confirmed and becomes part of scientific truth. If the idea does not work for other scientists the way it did for scientist A, the original research has to be repeated and checked until an error is found.

Some people say that science is "self-correcting" because errors will always be found out. Suppose a scientist makes up the result of an experiment. Other scientists who try to use those results will discover that they are false. Errors and dishonest reports cannot, therefore, survive for long in science. At least, that's what the rules of science predict. We'll discover later that this may not always be the case.

DECIDING ON RIGHT AND WRONG IN SCIENCE

Ethical problems have concerned men and women almost from the moment humans first began studying the natural world in a systematic way. The ethical code which doctors recite when they join the medical profession today goes back at least two thousand years. The Hippocratic oath defines what ethical behavior is when a physician works with his or her patients. The oath describes not only the methods that doctors should and should not use in treating the ill, but also the code of conduct they should follow in working with patients. One part of the code says, for example, "Whatever, in connection with my professional practice, or not in connection with it, I see or hear, in the life of men, which ought not to be spoken of abroad, I will not divulge as reckoning that all such should be kept secret."[1]

Perhaps the most famous historical example of an ethical dilemma in science comes from the life of the Swedish inventor Alfred Nobel. In 1866, Nobel discovered the explosive called dynamite. The discovery of dynamite made Nobel's fortune. He died in 1896, a multimillionaire . . . but also a troubled man.

Nobel realized the terrible weapon of war he had given the world. At one time, he thought that the use of dynamite in battle would produce so much devastation that the nations of the world would begin to find ways other than war to settle their differences. "Perhaps," he wrote, "my [dynamite] factories will end war sooner than your [peace] congresses. On the day when two army corps will be able to annihilate each other in one second, all civilized nations will recoil from war in horror and disband their forces."[2]

In the years following his discovery of dynamite, Nobel was constantly troubled by the ethical implications of what he had done. In the end, was his discovery a "good" or "bad" thing for human civilization? Was the positive ben-

efit of having a powerful new construction tool greater than the negative risk of greater pain and suffering from the use of dynamite in warfare?

Of course, each person would answer that question in his or her own way. Part of Nobel's answer was to leave his entire fortune, some $8 million, to the betterment of human society. In his will, he established a trust fund with this money from which to award prizes in literature, the sciences, and the pursuit of peace. These Nobel Prizes were one man's way of resolving the ethical questions raised by his accomplishments in science.

ETHICAL ISSUES IN SCIENCE TODAY

Even though scientists overall have no *formal* code of ethics, they do have an informal understanding about the right way to do research. (Some scientific societies *do* have formal codes, however.) The scientific community has, over many years, come to agree upon certain ethically acceptable procedures for doing and reporting on research.

Still, ethical issues in science are seldom clear-cut, black-and-white issues. Even though a scientist may know what colleagues think is the right way to do things, he or she may choose to do something else. Other factors may make, for this individual scientist, this choice the ethically correct one.

For example, suppose that a scientist is eager to work on an important military project for the government because he or she believes it will greatly strengthen the nation's defensive position. Taking part in the project is, for this scientist, an act of patriotism.

Alfred Nobel

But one condition of working on the project might be that the scientist cannot communicate research results to other scientists; the project is classified as "top secret." This would be a violation of one part of the scientific community's informal code of ethics that says that all research results must always be shared with all other members of the scientific community. In this case, certain considerations (national security) may convince a scientist to act in a way (suppressing information) that other scientists might normally think of as unethical.

Ethical dilemmas such as this one have become more important for scientists in recent years because of the vastly expanded role of science in our everyday lives. Today, scientists have to think not just about the way their actions will affect the scientific community, but what impact they will have on the community at large.

The case of the military researcher illustrates this point. He or she may decide to ignore one of the ethical tenets of science because social, economic, political, or other factors seem more important in this particular case.

Thus, we see today an increasing number of people, both inside and outside the scientific community, having to think about ethical implications of scientific research. Consider just a few of the issues about which you may have heard or read:

- If scientists are able to make larger and more powerful nuclear weapons, should they continue to do so, without limit?

- If scientists learn how to control the expression of genetic characteristics (genetic disease, hair color, intelligence, etc.), is there any point at which they should go no further with such research?

- What obligations do scientists have to report on incomplete, incorrect, or fraudulent research done by their colleagues?

"Well, we've finally isolated the gamma-mu anti-meson, and there don't seem to be—thank God!— any practical applications."

- Do scientists have the right to spend public tax dollars on "pure" research, such as research on planets or in outer space, that seems to have no promise of improving life on Earth?

Scientists are not always eager to take part in this debate on ethics. Most have been trained to believe that science operates according to a rather strict set of rules that govern their research. When those rules conflict with social, political, economic, legal, religious, and moral factors, they would prefer to let other members of society work out the conflict.

But ignoring their part in this debate has become more and more difficult for scientists. In some cases, like that of the scientist faced with a decision about participating in military research, the issue just *can't* be ignored. In other cases, scientists are simply beginning to see that they have an ethical responsibility to help resolve issues. For one thing, the kinds of research that scientists choose to do and the kinds of discoveries they make often determine the social and political issues of the next decade.

Also, scientists simply have too much technical knowledge in the field to leave these decisions entirely to politicians, religious leaders, sociologists, and other citizens. Understanding and solving modern social, political, and economic issues requires, therefore, the active participation of scientists.

In still other cases, nonscientists are *forcing* scientists to become involved in ethical debates. Some nonscientists have, for example, challenged certain types of research projects in the courts—and won! When this happens, scientists have no choice but to pay more attention to the social and ethical implications of their work.

This book provides some insight into the new ways that scientists are exploring an important new aspect of their profession, the questions of right and wrong raised by their work.

2

SCIENTIFIC RESEARCH

DR. CHU'S DILEMMA

Friday, October 11, is a critical date in the life of Dr. Henry Chu. On that date Dr. Chu must submit his proposal for financial support to the National Council for Scientific Research (NCSR). The funds Dr. Chu seeks are crucial to the continuation of his research. Dr. Chu has been working on a technique to cure the common cold and believes that he is very close to having solved this problem. But he badly needs additional money to spend one more year on his research.

As he works on his request for funding, Dr. Chu faces some tough decisions. He realizes that the NCSR will approve his proposal only if it believes he has made significant progress on his research so far. Therefore, Dr. Chu needs to describe his research in the most favorable light possible. He wants to show that his new technique really does offer a cure for the common cold.

However, Dr. Chu also realizes that his research results are not completely positive. In about 70 percent of his cases, patients have been cured by Dr. Chu's treatment. In about 20 percent of the cases, the patients were no better and no worse. And in about 10 percent of the cases, his patients actually became sicker.

No matter that 30 percent of his subjects were *not* cured by his treatment, Dr. Chu is still quite certain that the treatment will ultimately work, or at least that it will cause no harm to the people who receive it. He can think of many reasons that the experimental treatments may have failed: perhaps patients did not take their medication properly or laboratory assistants made errors in their reports, for example.

Dr. Chu's dilemma is how to write a report that is honest, yet will describe his research in the most favorable light. The problem is that there is often more than one "honest" way to describe one's research. For legitimate reasons, a scientist might mention some results and omit others.

Exactly what should he say, Dr. Chu wonders, to fulfill his professional obligations as a scientist and still maximize his chances of getting the NCSR grant?

SOME ETHICAL CHOICES FOR DR. CHU

Are you confused about Dr. Chu's situation? After all, scientists are expected to be completely honest, aren't they? And honesty means telling the truth, the whole truth, and nothing but the truth. If Dr. Chu is going to behave like a real scientist, then we might expect him to report *all* his research results, whether they support his ideas or not.

Besides, Dr. Chu knows how risky it is to tell less than the truth in science. His colleagues are likely to find out if he makes up information or publishes inaccurate or incomplete data.

On the other hand, an important part of Dr. Chu's career—past, present, and future—depends on his getting an NCSR grant. Dr. Chu realizes that a discovery as important as this one might earn him promotions at his university, worldwide recognition, even a Nobel Prize.

"Professor Ziegler's working on a way to get our research grant renewed."

Dr. Chu is not ignorant of the humanitarian benefits of his research. A successful treatment for the common cold could bring relief to millions of people every year. Successful completion of this research would be one of the great medical achievements of this century.

But if the NCSR review board is not impressed by Dr. Chu's results, they might decide not to give him any money. His project would come to an end, and any chance he had for fame and fortune would disappear. Perhaps most important, a vital step forward in medical research might be delayed for years.

One reason that Dr. Chu's situation is so difficult is the nature of scientific research itself. Experiments seldom produce clean, neat, simple results that have an obvious meaning to everyone. More commonly, they yield conflicting data that can be interpreted in more than one way. Maybe the negative results in Dr. Chu's experiment *can* be explained as he thinks they can. In that case, reporting the failed experiments might not really give a true picture of the research results. Perhaps he would be entirely justified in leaving out some of his less favorable data.

An interesting example of this point is found in Gregor Mendel's pioneering research on genetics in the mid-1800s. For many years, historians of science have wondered about the results Mendel published for his research on pea plants. Those experimental results were remarkably close to the theoretical results Mendel had predicted for his experiment. He seemed to have had no bad luck and made almost no errors in his research.

To some observers, Mendel's results were "too good to be true."[3] Some have even suggested that Mendel might have cheated a bit in writing his report, leaving out

Gregor Mendel experimenting with his famous pea plants

some results or adding in others that would make his overall results look better.

No one knows the answer to that question. But Dr. Mel Usselman of the University of Western Ontario has offered another interesting explanation for this situation.[4] Suppose Mendel *did* go through his data, choose those results that made the most sense to him, and ignore those which appeared to be the result of errors or "natural quirks." Suppose Mendel had, that is, selectively reported on his data rather than recording *all* of his results. Would that decision have made Mendel's work unethical?

Professor Usselman suggests that, on the contrary, Mendel's ability to recognize which data were significant and which insignificant may constitute the difference between an average or even good scientist and a great scientist. Mendel's greatness may not rest, he believes, on the careful experiments he carried out and the careful notes he took, but on his ability to see patterns in masses of data, patterns that might have escaped someone who was simply doing experiments and writing out every last result.

In summary, the issue facing Dr. Chu—and the issue that faces many other scientists—arises because some ethical choices in science are not black and white. The question may not be simply to choose between a "right" action and a "wrong" action. Instead, gray areas exist where no clear "correct" action is obvious. Describe these situations to ten scientists, and you might get five answers as to the ethically proper decision to make.

At least three situations commonly exist in which scientists must choose among alternative actions:

1. Deciding which experimental data one will include in a research report
2. Giving (or not giving) credit to colleagues and co-workers for their ideas and experimental work
3. Allowing nonscientific factors (such as personal

biases) to determine the research projects one does and the ways in which that research is interpreted.

"FUDGING" ON RESEARCH RESULTS

Dr. Chu's dilemma illustrates the first of the situations listed above. What results should (must) he leave in his proposal and what results should (could) he leave out? As mentioned, this problem arises partly because of the nature of scientific research itself. Experiments seldom produce neat, clean answers that are simple to interpret. Consider just two factors that might affect the way an experiment comes out.

First, a scientist might have made an error: added too much of a chemical, read a meter incorrectly, or left a burner on too long, for example. In many cases, the scientist might never realize that the error had been made until the experiment was over, if then.

Second, the longer a scientist uses a particular technique, the more proficient he or she becomes with it. We might normally expect, then, that the hundredth repetition of an experiment would yield better results than would the second or third repetition.

When Dr. Chu looks at the result of his cold treatment experiments, he would certainly *like* to believe that the 30 percent negative results came about as the result of experimental errors. He might be tempted simply not to mention those results in his grant proposal. If he could honestly do so, the proposal would look a great deal better.

Besides, if Professor Usselman is correct, Dr. Chu may have an *obligation* to exercise his professional judgment about the best way to report his data. Who is likely to recognize which results are significant and which not significant better than Dr. Chu?

"The stuff's perfectly safe. We tested it on our animal subjects and none of them show any ill effects whatsoever."

Picking and choosing among experimental results, as Dr. Chu may do in this example, is common in science. The practice is often referred to as "fudging the results" or "massaging the data." Would Dr. Chu be acting unethically if he massaged his data? No simple answer to that question exists. On the one hand, he will certainly be motivated by the desire to give his results the best possible appearance. His career prospects, his standing in the scientific community, his social position in the general community, and his standard of living will probably all benefit from strong, positive results in his experiments.

On the other hand, Dr. Chu can hardly disregard his professional commitment to complete honesty (whatever that means in this case) in whatever choices he makes.

But other factors may be involved in Dr. Chu's decision, too. Should he omit results for which he can find no errors just because they detract from the success of his work? Should he leave out results that might, in fact, have some harmful effect on the health of people in the community? Suppose his negative results are not caused by errors, but really show that the treatment has dangerous side effects on some people. Can and should he really leave out and ignore these results of his research?

The one action Dr. Chu might be tempted to take which other scientists would almost certainly see as clearly unethical is to invent data or describe experiments that never took place. It would be difficult, if not impossible, for most scientists to understand *any* reason that a fellow scientist would report on an experiment that he or she hadn't done, create data rather than provide them from actual observation, or fail to report results which he or she *knows* are important.

The interesting point, however, is that instances of outright fraud in science are not so uncommon as you might expect. In some situations, personal, economic, professional, and other pressures appear to have been so strong as to cause scientists to lie and cheat about their work even though they probably knew in advance that other scientists would regard such behavior as unethical and possibly illegal.

ALTERING DATA IN THE INTEREST OF NATIONAL SECURITY

The pressure to massage one's research results sometimes come from forces outside a scientist's own research or personal life. Such a situation arose in early 1986 when officials from the U.S. Navy began to question research being done by the National Oceanic and Atmospheric Administration (NOAA).

NOAA scientists were using highly sophisticated methods for mapping 3.9 billion acres of ocean floor around the United States. The NOAA project promised to yield by far the most precise ocean bottom maps ever produced. These maps would be of enormous value to petroleum companies, fishermen, companies looking for minerals on the ocean bottoms and researchers from many fields of science.

The Navy's concern about the NOAA project was that the new maps might fall into the hands of an enemy. With access to these maps, enemy submarines would be able to navigate and maneuver in U.S. coastal waters with an efficiency and safety they do not now have.

One way of handling this problem suggested by the Navy was for NOAA to release the new maps in "coded" form. Various segments could be printed in a rotated or slightly altered form in order to confuse agents of an unfriendly nation.[5] In effect, the Navy was asking NOAA to "massage" its new map data in the interest of national security.

Some scientists could understand and agree with the reasons for making these changes. Clearly, an enemy with the new, better maps would be a greater threat to our nation. But would NOAA be justified in releasing to the scientific community slightly altered maps? Would the inconvenience and errors in the published versions be justified by concern for national security?

USING THE WORK OF OTHERS

A second issue that may arise as scientists report on their research is how to make use of discoveries and ideas made by other scientists. Again, the nature of scientific research itself creates some problems here.

Every idea in science builds on other ideas that went before it. One of the greatest of all scientists, Sir Isaac Newton, expressed this principle when he said that he had been able to accomplish so much only because he had been "standing on the shoulders of Giants." That is, he recognized that his successes depended at least partly on the work of scientists who had gone before him. It's simply understood that scientists will always give credit to others who have thought about and developed ideas on any subject.

Yet, some of the ideas that scientists develop are truly more significant than others. Newton may have used the ideas of many earlier scientists in developing his theory of gravitation. But the way in which he put those ideas together and the new way of looking at those ideas that Newton suggested made his contributions revolutionary. The world will always acknowledge that Newton's ideas about gravitational attraction were very special indeed.

Many scientists want to develop that kind of very special idea that sets them apart from their colleagues. Why? Again, an accomplishment such as this can bring wealth, career advancement, and recognition from other scientists and from the world at large.

On occasion, the desire to become a success in

science is so great that a scientist will even steal someone else's ideas without giving that person credit. The theft of someone else's work or ideas is called plagiarism. Plagiarism is illegal in most legal systems of the world.

The history of science contains some interesting chapters about individuals who have advanced in their profession by stealing the work of others. An Iraqi "scientist" by the name of Elias Alsabti managed to fool the scientific establishment in the United States, Jordan, and his native country for over five years. He managed to publish about sixty research papers, all stolen from other scientists' work. Although he achieved modest recognition in his brief career, he is not known to have done any original research.[6]

GIVING CREDIT WHERE CREDIT IS DUE

Outright plagiarism is seldom an ethical issue for scientists. They know that colleagues will condemn plagiarism as unethical and society will call their behavior illegal. But decisions of when and to what extent a scientist should give credit to other scientists can still be difficult and ethically unclear at times. For example, a scientist writing a research report knows that he or she is expected to give credit to anyone whose ideas have appeared in print (in journal articles, for example).

But scientists present their ideas in other contexts also. For example, they give speeches, write personal letters, and have informal conversations at professional meetings. In situations such as these, the ideas that scientists talk about are often still being formulated. Scientists share their thoughts with colleagues in order to get feedback, to find out if they are on the right track with regard to an idea.

To what extent do scientists have to acknowledge ideas they have heard about in informal settings such as these? Suppose that another scientist in a different country is also working on the same research project as Dr. Chu's. And suppose that this scientist has made a crucial suggestion which Dr. Chu has used in his own research. Does Dr. Chu have to give credit for that suggestion? Or can he say that he thought of the idea on his own?

We might be tempted to say that all scientists should always acknowledge all ideas they get from other scientists. That might sound as though it would solve a scientist's ethical dilemma here. But that's an overly simplified and unrealistic solution to his problem. In the first place, scientists are often not honestly able to say where their ideas originally came from. They may simply not be able to say whether the idea developed out of their own research and thinking or whether it came as a result of talking with colleagues and reading about their work.

Besides, we don't live in a perfect world where everyone always *wants* to do exactly what's absolutely pure and honest. We can imagine that a scientist will want to receive a large share of the credit for any new discovery he or she makes. For truly significant discoveries there is normally only one Nobel Prize and a few other honors.

In many cases, a scientist may honestly believe that he or she *deserves* and *has earned* that credit. Scientists know when they have made truly significant breakthroughs in their field. They know when they have earned the right to "go down in history" as an important figure in their discipline. Why should they lose or share that recognition? Doesn't a scientist have the right to make a strong case for his or her priority in making a discovery?

So the way scientists finally acknowledge the work of others in their research reports is often a fine balance among what they know they *must do* (mentioning the written reports of others), what they think they *can do* to maximize their own contributions, and what they believe they *ought to do* as an ethical acknowledgment of the work of others.

THE SPECIAL PROBLEM OF GRADUATE STUDENTS

Proper recognition of another's scientific work can also become an issue when the work of graduate students is involved. Who gets the credit for an idea developed by a student working in the laboratory of an older scientist who has provided the intellectual, financial, and social support for the student's research?

This issue arises often in science because one of the steps that all scientists go through in becoming full-fledged, accepted members of the scientific community involves one or more years of graduate study. During their graduate study, students take courses and do an original research project. The research project takes place under the direction of a university professor, the student's *graduate adviser*.

In most cases, the graduate adviser helps the student develop the student's research ideas. However, the adviser may actually suggest a project connected with the adviser's work. The adviser also provides the graduate student with financial support (often paying university tuition and other expenses), a laboratory to work in, and the equipment needed for research. The adviser's professional connections are often crucial, also, in helping the student to get a job after graduation.

So who "owns" an idea developed by a graduate student working in a setting such as this? Suppose that one of Dr. Chu's students, for example, invented a very important step in his method of treating colds. We may be able to say that the idea was really the student's own. But would that idea have been developed without the aid and cooperation of the student's adviser, Dr. Chu?

It might be to Dr. Chu's benefit to claim as much credit for his student's work as possible. And, given his support of the student's work, perhaps that would be a fair decision.

But then is it fair to the student to ignore his or her

A medical student doing research at a hospital lab

contributions to Dr. Chu's research? After all, the student really did the work necessary to develop the idea and probably should have at least some share of the credit.

A classic example of this problem was the research on diabetes carried out by Frederick Banting and Charles Best in the early 1920s.[7] Best, a medical student at the time, was assigned to work with Dr. Banting by his adviser, John J. R. Macleod. In addition, Dr. Macleod provided laboratory space for Banting and Best to carry out their experiment.

As a result of their research, Banting and Best learned that people with diabetes lacked the essential chemical insulin. Providing insulin to these people helped them overcome the worst aspects of this disease. When the Nobel Prize for this discovery was awarded, however, it went to Banting and Macleod, not to the graduate student Best, who, with Banting, actually did all the research work.

Was it ethical for Dr. Macleod to have accepted this award? What ethical dilemma did Dr. Banting face in this situation?

The elements of the Banting-Best-Macleod story still exist today. No generally accepted guidelines exist to tell advisers how much credit to give their students and in what way to provide that credit. Some scientists, in fact, use their graduate students as "slave labor" from whom they extract as much personal glory and recognition as possible. They may sign research reports of students who work under them although they have taken no active part in the research itself. On the other hand, many graduate advisers are known for the generosity with which they provide credit to their students.

Banting (right) and Best, the discoverers of insulin, with one of the first diabetic dogs they treated

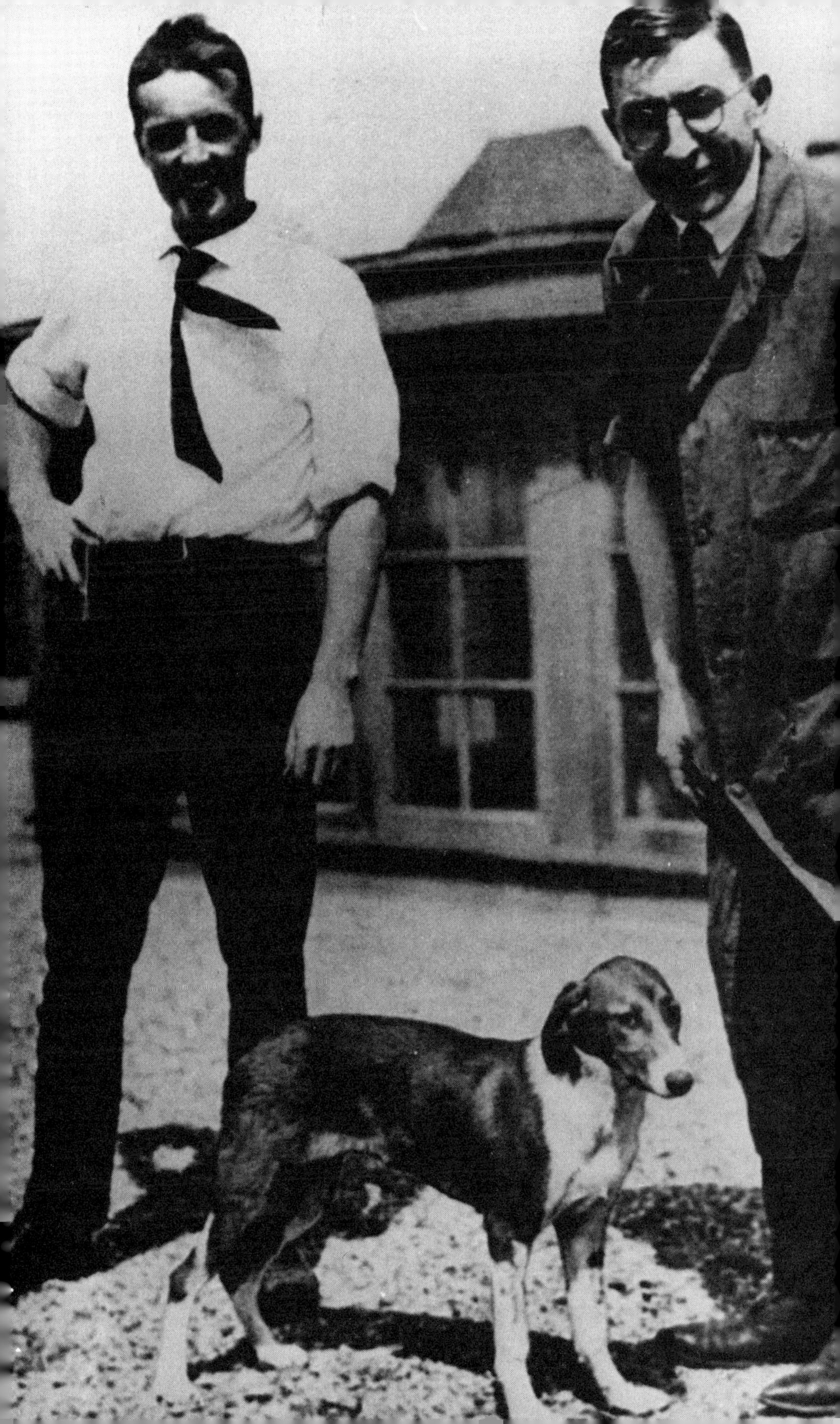

OBJECTIVITY IN SCIENCE AND ETHICAL CHOICES

A critical rule in the game of science is that researchers must always be *objective*. What we mean by objectivity in science is that a researcher does not allow private attitudes, beliefs, feelings, hopes, or expectations to affect the outcome or interpretation of an experiment. Objectivity means simply choosing a research project, doing an experiment, observing the results, and then reporting on those results without being influenced by personal factors.

The opposite of objectivity, *subjectivity*, means that scientists allow their racial attitudes, political allegiances, hopes for social change, or other nonscientific factors to affect the way they do an experiment or the way they interpret and report their research.

But the goal of perfect objectivity in science, although a noble one, is probably too much to hope for anyway. For example, scientists do not decide *at random* what research they will work on. They have special areas of interest and expertise which partially determine the experiments they choose to do. Neither are they likely to be absolutely neutral as to how their research turns out. Scientists, like the rest of us, want to have success in their work, want to have their ideas confirmed. And few scientists are so totally objective and so totally disinterested in the results of their work that they don't care what influence, if any, their research will have on the rest of the world. However, most scientists do not try to change the actual outcome of their research.

So, in actual practice, much scientific research is likely to contain at least some elements of its director's personal, subjective feelings, ambitions, and expectations. And the more directly that research deals with important social and political issues, the more significant those feelings, ambitions, and expectations are likely to be.

We probably would not expect the personal philosophy of a scientist with radical socialist (or conservative authoritarian) biases to have much effect if his or her research concerns the internal composition of stars. But that philosophy could make a difference if the scientist's specialty is motivational psychology, the study of ways to influence people's behavior.

Therefore, it can sometimes be difficult to make the distinction between a reasonable level of subjectivity in research (scientists choosing the work they like to do and think is important and then hoping that it will come out well) and a level of subjectivity which leads scientists to use questionable research methods and ways of reporting.

SOME EXAMPLES OF SUBJECTIVITY IN SCIENCE

Some of the most interesting and troubling stories for the history of scientific ethics involve the work of scientists who have gone too far in allowing personal biases to affect their research. In some cases (as may be commonly true), these scientists may not even have realized that they were being subjective.

For example, many medical researchers at the end of the last century seemed to have held certain preconceived notions (biases) about women, especially with regard to what was "normal" and "natural" feminine behavior. Passivity, lack of interest in intellectual matters, and dependence were three qualities these "experts" regarded as "natural feminine traits."

When these researchers actually worked with women, they often seemed to make their research results fit their preconceived notions. A strong, assertive, independent woman was usually seen, for example, not as a piece of evidence that the researchers might be wrong about "natural feminine traits." Instead, she was probably explained as a "deviant" female who needed psychological therapy or medical treatment.

Many scientists and historians today look back at the way nineteenth-century medical scientists thought about and treated women and their "problems," and they are shocked at their colleagues' lack of objectivity. More than that, they recognize the personal harm that this "scientific" attitude had on many women.[8]

Had these earlier scientists behaved ethically in their studies and treatment of women? Of course, we can't look back into the minds of those nineteenth-century men and try to understand what their thoughts, motives, and logic were. Still, from reading their writings, we get the impression that they *thought* they were acting in a fair, unbiased, and completely scientific way when they wrote about and treated women. Perhaps their own biases were so ingrained that they never saw how powerfully their personal prejudices had affected the objectivity of their scientific work.

Unfortunately, attitudes such as these even among professional scientists or doctors have not completely died out even today. Some scientists seem *knowingly* to have allowed their personal prejudices to affect their scientific work. One of the most dramatic examples of this is the case of Sir Cyril Burt.[9]

Sir Cyril has been called one of the greatest psychologists of the twentieth century. He was knighted by King George VI in 1946 for his studies of intelligence.

Sir Cyril believed strongly that a person's intelligence resulted primarily from heredity (what was passed down from his or her parents) rather than environment (what was learned after birth). He produced a number of books, wrote hundreds of scholarly papers, gave untold numbers of public addresses, and served on many important committees, always arguing for the role of heredity over environment in determining intelligence.

Sir Cyril apparently felt so strongly about his ideas that

he actually invented a number of experiments to support his beliefs. He created data and made up co-workers to whom he referred in his books, articles, and speeches. The purpose of his fraud was apparently to make even more convincing his beliefs of the role of heredity in determining intelligence.

After Burt's death in 1971, other researchers began to realize that some important parts of his research were fabricated. The co-workers whom he mentioned were never found, and some of the numbers he reported for experiments were shown to have been falsified. Many scientists were quick to label his actions as both dishonest and unethical.

The case of Sir Cyril Burt illustrates the ways in which dishonesty in science can have enormous social, political, economic, and other consequences. Through his writings and speeches, Burt strongly influenced the shape that British education was to take in the middle third of the twentieth century. The suggestions he made and the educational structures which developed were based, it now appears, on false or nonexistent scientific data. The unethical decisions Burt made more than half a century ago continue to exert their influence on the educational system followed by British boys and girls today.

SCIENCE AND ETHICS: EVERYONE'S CONCERN

These two examples illustrate the point that nonscientists like you and me, as well as professional scientists, sometimes may want to become involved in discussions of ethical issues in science. In both of these caes, scientists tried to influence social attitudes, educational practices, and political policy through their research, their treatments, and their public statements. Yet, members of the general public may not have been (and probably *were* not) aware of the scientists' personal "axes to grind" in each case.

Imagine, for example, how different the lives of some women might have been had the general public realized in the nineteenth century that the statements many physicians were making about "proper feminine behavior" were statements of personal bias and not scientific knowledge!

Many of us tend to respect scientists and to expect them to be honest and objective in their work. So we may find it difficult to realize that these people occasionally use their research to promote their own social, political, economic, religious, or personal goals.

The lesson we can learn from these examples is to look carefully at those instances in which scientists suggest that *our* attitudes, practices, and policies ought to be consistent with *their* research. In such cases, we may want to know more about their own personal biases and prejudices—their own lack of objectivity—as scientists.

Some of the topics covered later in this book, genetic engineering and weapons research, for example, are the kinds of issues in which scientific objectivity is especially important. In public debates on topics such as these, nonscientists as well as scientists have a crucial role in examining the ethics of scientific research and recommendations.

3

RESEARCH ON ANIMALS AND HUMANS

DR. MILNER'S DILEMMA

Dr. Andrew Milner sometimes wonders if he cares *too much* about animals. His friends often joke about "his family" of two dogs, three cats, two hamsters, and four finches. They say his pets get more attention and better care than many human children.

Now Dr. Milner's love for animals is being tested at his job. His supervisor at the Kwal-l-T Testing Company has assigned him a project that requires the use of rabbits in an experiment. The experiment involves a series of tests using Eye-Brite, a new kind of eye-liner developed by Cosmetics International (CI). CI wants to know if its new eye-liner will cause any harm to women who use the product.

Dr. Milner's boss has decided that the best way to test Eye-Brite is to place the cosmetic directly into the eyes of rabbits. Then, the rabbits are to be observed over a period of four weeks to see if they develop any infections or experience any other medical problems.

Dr. Milner understands the importance of this experiment to CI. The company would not want to be responsible for a new product until it had been tested and found safe. The program Dr. Milner is expected to carry out is a standard procedure in science.

Still, he is unhappy about the way the experiment has been designed. He suspects that the rabbits will suffer serious discomfort and may experience considerable pain. He's not sure that having a new cosmetic is worth the agony the experimental animals may have to suffer.

THE PROS AND CONS OF ANIMAL EXPERIMENTATION

The choice facing Dr. Milner is a common one in many fields of science. Under what circumstances, if any, is it ethical to use animals in research? What arguments are there for inflicting pain, discomfort, and even death on experimental animals? For what reasons should animals *not* be used in research? Should humans participate in research? If so, are the ethical choices the same for humans as they are for laboratory animals?

For many scientists, the arguments for using experimental animals are clear. Companies that produce drugs, pesticides, food additives, cosmetics, and other new products must be sure that their products are safe for use by humans. They also want to find out if the products do the things they are intended to do.

Scientists usually get this information by means of a two-step process. First, experiments are carried out on laboratory animals—rats, mice, hamsters, chimpanzees, dogs, and cats, for example. Then, based on the results of these tests, additional experiments on humans may (or may not) be carried out.

This practice raises two questions: First, is it ethical to do research on laboratory animals? Second, is it ethical to do research on humans? Many scientists say that the answer to the first of these question is yes.[10] They see the choice as between the value of human life and the value of

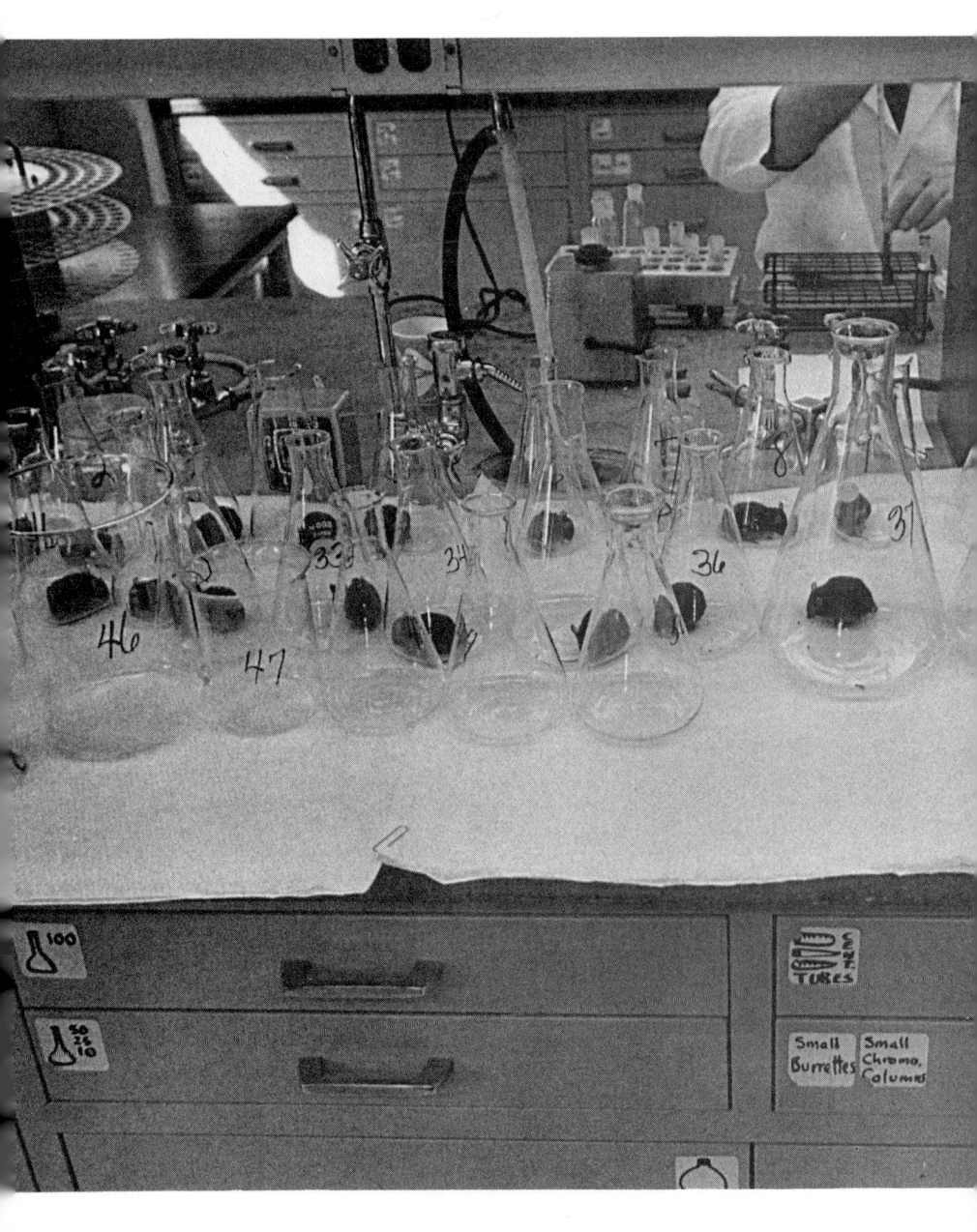

Experimental mice in a cancer research lab

a rat's (or some other laboratory animal's) life. They may feel justified in sacrificing the health, comfort, and (perhaps) life of animals in order to bring better commercial products to human society. By using laboratory animals, these researchers are saying in effect that they believe a human life has more worth than the life of a rat, a chimp, a dog, or a cat.

Other scientists and laypersons disagree.[11] They argue that *all* life is equally sacred. Human life is not special and should not be favored over the lives of other animals. Thus, these individuals believe, rats, chimps, or dogs have certain rights just like those of humans. The 1977 "Declaration against Speciesism" summarizes this position:

Inasmuch as we believe that there is ample evidence that many other species are capable of feeling, we condemn totally the infliction of suffering upon our brother animals, and the curtailment of their enjoyment, unless it be necessary for their own individual benefit.

We do not accept that a difference in species alone (any more than a difference in race) can justify wanton exploitation or oppression in the name of science or sport, or for food, commercial profit or other human gain.

We believe in the evolutionary and moral kinship of all animals, and we declare our belief that all sentient creatures have rights to life, liberty, and the quest for happiness.

We call for the protection of these rights.

WHEN TO USE ANIMALS IN RESEARCH

Most scientists are probably willing to say that laboratory animals should be used in experiments under certain circumstances. What circumstances might justify the use of animals in research?

"It's most interesting. By pushing
this lever twenty times you can get him
to walk across here with a banana."

"Do you know a good malpractice lawyer?"

For one thing, the kind of animals to be used may be an important consideration. Many people seem to feel that animals most like humans (chimpanzees, for example) or most a part of our lives (dogs and cats) deserve more consideration in research. These people tend to believe that experiments involving rats and mice may be all right to do, but experiments involving apes and dogs are not.

The ethical argument here seems to be, once more, that the lives of some kinds of animals (chimps and dogs, for example) are worth more than those of other kinds (rats and mice, for example). The knowledge we gain in an experiment using rats and mice, then, is more important and more valuable than the lives of those animals.

Another consideration is the kind of experiment to be carried out. Suppose Dr. Milner's assignment had been to test a new anticancer drug rather than a new cosmetic. Then, he might have felt more justified in doing tests on rabbits. The results of his research could mean relief from pain and suffering and perhaps life itself for countless humans. The choice now would be between the pain caused some rabbits in an experiment compared to the potentially great benefit to humans. In contrast, Dr. Milner's present choice is between the suffering he will cause his rabbits versus the availability of a new cosmetic.

A final ethical question scientists sometimes have to consider is the availability of other ways of testing new products. In recent years, scientists have developed testing methods that require the use of fewer experimental animals. For example, some computer programs exist that respond to drugs in much the same way that humans respond. A researcher can feed information about a new drug into one of these programs, and the computer will decide how a human would react to that drug.

But no computer program is foolproof. What if the information that comes out of the computer is incomplete or wrong? Concern about this possibility prompts many researchers to continue using experimental animals over computer programs or other alternatives. The pain and suffering caused the animals is still a small price to pay, they reason, compared to the benefits their research will bring to humans.

USING HUMANS IN RESEARCH

Dr. Milner's ethical dilemma about experimenting with rabbits could have been much more difficult. Suppose he had been asked to use humans in his research. Would it have been ethical for him to test Eye-Brite in the eyes of men and women, boys and girls? What arguments *for* and *against* this decision would Dr. Milner have had to consider?

The major reason for using humans in an experiment such as this one is a practical one. No one can be *sure* about the effects of a drug, pesticide, food additive, or cosmetic on humans from animal experiments alone. A researcher always has to ask whether a human will react to a new product in exactly the same way that a rat, a chimp, or a dog has.

One possibility, then, is to test a new product on human subjects to find out its effects. The researcher will then be able to say how safe and effective that product is *for humans*. The problem is that one can never predict perfectly from animal tests what the effects on the human research subjects will be.

Another possibility is to depend entirely on animal, computer, or other nonhuman studies of a new product. Then the health and lives of human subjects are not endangered, but a researcher cannot be positive about the product's subsequent effects on humans.

The ethical decision facing a scientist, then, involves weighing the potential benefits of knowing a product's effects on humans versus the potential dangers to human subjects in an experiment. The question is whether knowledge gained from an experiment is worth the risk that

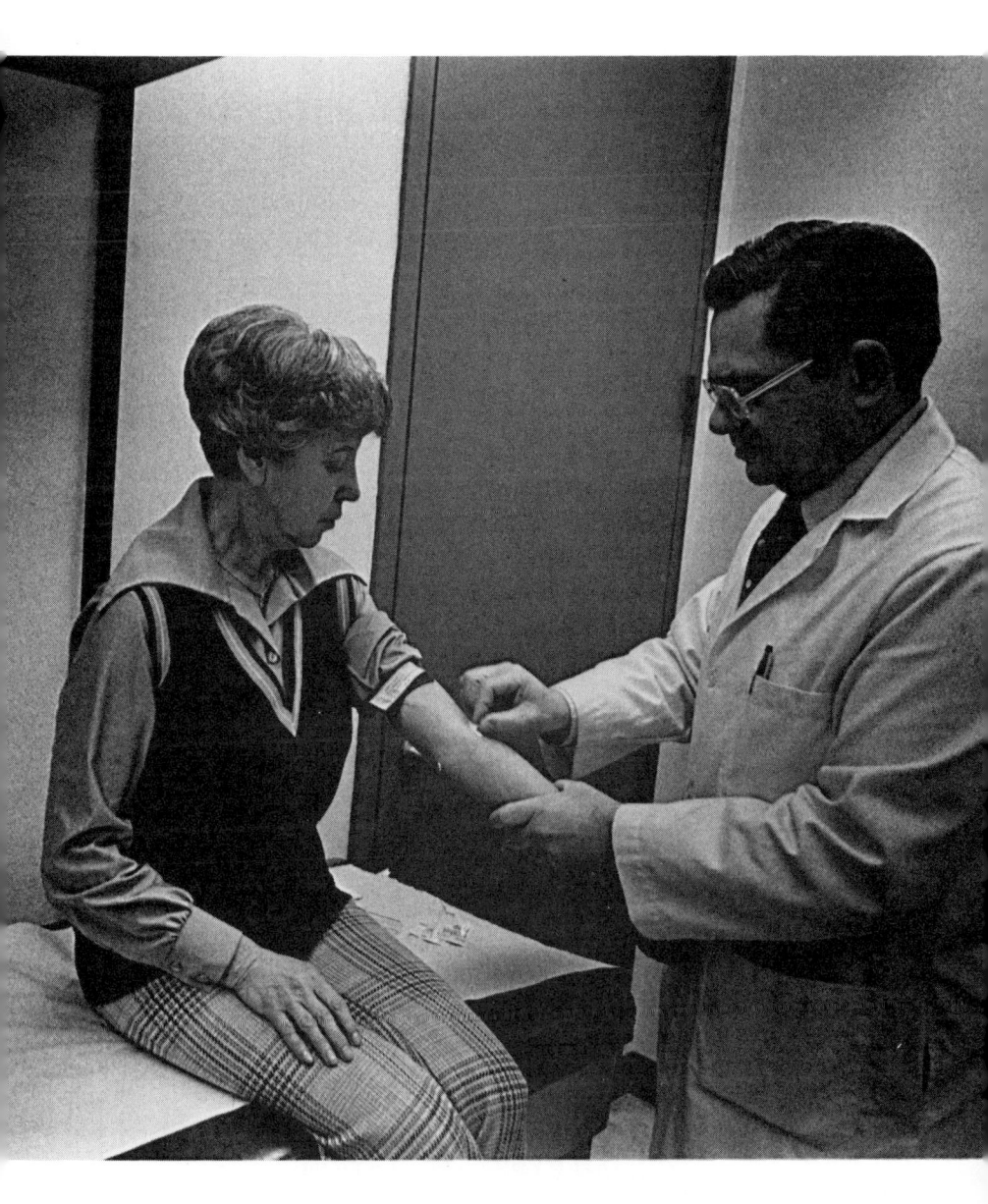

A volunteer in a genetics project at the Albert Einstein College of Medicine in Bronx, New York

human subjects might face in the research. Is it reasonable and ethical to ask subjects to put up with pain, nausea, and other discomforts to test a possible new cure for skin cancer?

The ethical problems involved in human experimentation are obvious to both scientists and laypersons. Today, research that uses human subjects must follow certain legal, professional, and ethical guidelines. First, scientists may use only *volunteers* for such experiments. No one can be forced to take part in an experiment if he or she doesn't want to.

Second, volunteers must give their *informed consent* to the experiment. Informed consent means that a person knows what an experiment is about, understands the risks and benefits involved, and fully agrees to take part in the research.

Informed consent helps a scientist make ethical choices. It means that the human subject has weighed the pros and cons of taking part in the experiment. By agreeing to participate, the subject seems to acknowledge that the good that may come from the experiment to himself, herself, or another human is of greater value than any harm he or she may experience.

Third, experiments involving human subjects must be approved by committees of other scientists and laypersons. Scientists who want to use human volunteers must describe to these committees the nature of their research, the kind of testing that will be done on subjects, and the safeguards built into the experiment. And they must provide evidence that the subjects really are volunteers.

ARGUMENTS AGAINST HUMAN EXPERIMENTATION

Arguments also can be made against the use of humans in research. For one thing, the good that comes from an experiment may not justify the dangers to a person's safe-

"I suppose the NSPCC *(a British regulatory agency)* will be the next lot to complain."

ty, health, and life. For example, suppose that Dr. Milner *had* decided to test Eye-Brite on humans. His dilemma, then, would have been to weigh the potential value of a new cosmetic against the dangers his experiment might have posed for human subjects. Would it have been worth causing eye infections in thirty human subjects in order to learn about the safety of Eye-Brite? Even approval from a review committee might not have resolved this problem for Dr. Milner. Even under the best plans with the best knowledge available, unexpected side effects might still result.

Questions sometimes arise also about the use of informed consent. How can a scientist be sure that his or her potential subjects *really* understand the risks of an experiment and agree to participate of *their own free will*?

Imagine, for example, that scientists would like to test a new drug for the treatment of Alzheimer's disease. This condition, which may afflict millions of Americans, involves the slow but progressive loss of one's mental abilities. Most patients who would be the best subjects for this research have mental abilities of a two- or three-year-old child. They probably could not understand what the experiment was all about.

Researchers can (and do) ask permission to use a patient in research from spouses, children, other relatives, and family physicians. But is it right for them to ask these individuals? And is it right for one person to give permission for someone else to be used in an experiment?

Another concern about the use of humans in experiments is how and why potential subjects give their "free" consent. For example, scientists who work for the military sometimes get human subjects for their research from members of the armed forces. The question is how freely a soldier or a prisoner is likely to agree to be part of an experiment. We sometimes hear how "volunteers" are obtained in the military. Is it right for scientists to use "volunteers" such as these in their research?

Medical researchers often face another issue. As physicians (as many of them are) and scientists, is their primary responsibility to heal their patients or to gain more knowledge about a particular medical problem?

For example, suppose that a new surgical method for the control of obesity has become available. The procedure involves closing off a portion of a person's stomach. The hope is that patients with smaller stomachs will have reduced appetites, will eat less, and will lose weight. Scientists might like to find out if this procedure is more or less successful than dieting, hypnosis, or other methods of weight control.

One way to answer this question might be to find thirty obese volunteers for an experiment. Half of these volunteers would have the new surgical procedure done; the other half would have no surgery. The second (control) group would receive no special treatment for their obesity.

Is the physician-scientist acting ethically to *all* of the subjects in this experiment? Is he or she sacrificing proper treatment for those in the control group in order to answer the research question? Can he or she argue that the health problems of a few obese people in the control group can be ignored while a (possibly) successful treatment for other obese people is being tested?

4

GENETIC RESEARCH

DR. GROTH'S DILEMMA

The Department of Biochemistry at Weldun University is an exciting place to be these days. Dr. Vernon Groth, department chairman, has just produced a new form of bacterium that can digest plastic. The new organism was produced by altering the genetic structure of *E. coli*, a common bacterium found in the human stomach.

Dr. Groth found a way to remove a key compound from the bacterium, change the chemical structure of that compound, and then reinsert the altered compound into the bacterium. The altered bacterium is different from the original bacterium in one important way: It can "eat" plastic.

Dr. Groth's discovery has enormous potential for helping to solve the nation's waste disposal problem. Currently, about 10 percent of all solid wastes in the United States consist of plastic products. These products do not decay, as do waste paper, foods, and other forms of trash. Instead, they stay in the soil essentially forever.

The next step in Dr. Groth's research would normally be to study the behavior of the new bacterium in nature. He currently plans to release a sample of the bacterium at a waste disposal site near the university, where he can observe its effect on plastics.

However, objections to Dr. Groth's research have begun to surface in the general public. People living near the trash site have expressed concern that their health and safety may be endangered by Dr. Groth's research. They want Dr. Groth's absolute assurance that the experiment will not harm them, their crops, or their animals.

This turn of events poses a difficult ethical problem for Dr. Groth. While he is personally confident that the new bacterium is safe for release, he knows that he cannot give such positive assurance at this point. Yet, he feels that he must continue his research on this new bacterium. He wonders what the most ethical solution to this problem is.

NEW KNOWLEDGE, NEW PROBLEMS

Dr. Groth's situation is familiar to many biologists today. In recent years, scientists have learned a lot about the way in which an organism's traits develop: how and why one horse has brown hair and another black, how and why some pea plants have tall stems and others short, how and why you have blue eyes and your sister has green.

The information an organism uses in developing these traits is stored in chemical structures called *genes*. Every cell in every plant, animal, and human contains thousands of genes that determine what they are like.

Scientists have also learned how to change the structure of genes. They can take genes out of an organism's body, change them chemically, and put them back into the organism. The changed genes carry different information and tell the organism to perform different funtions. This procedure is sometimes known as *genetic engineering*.

For example, we know that the human disease known as diabetes is caused by a defective gene. Using the knowledge they are now developing, scientists will some-

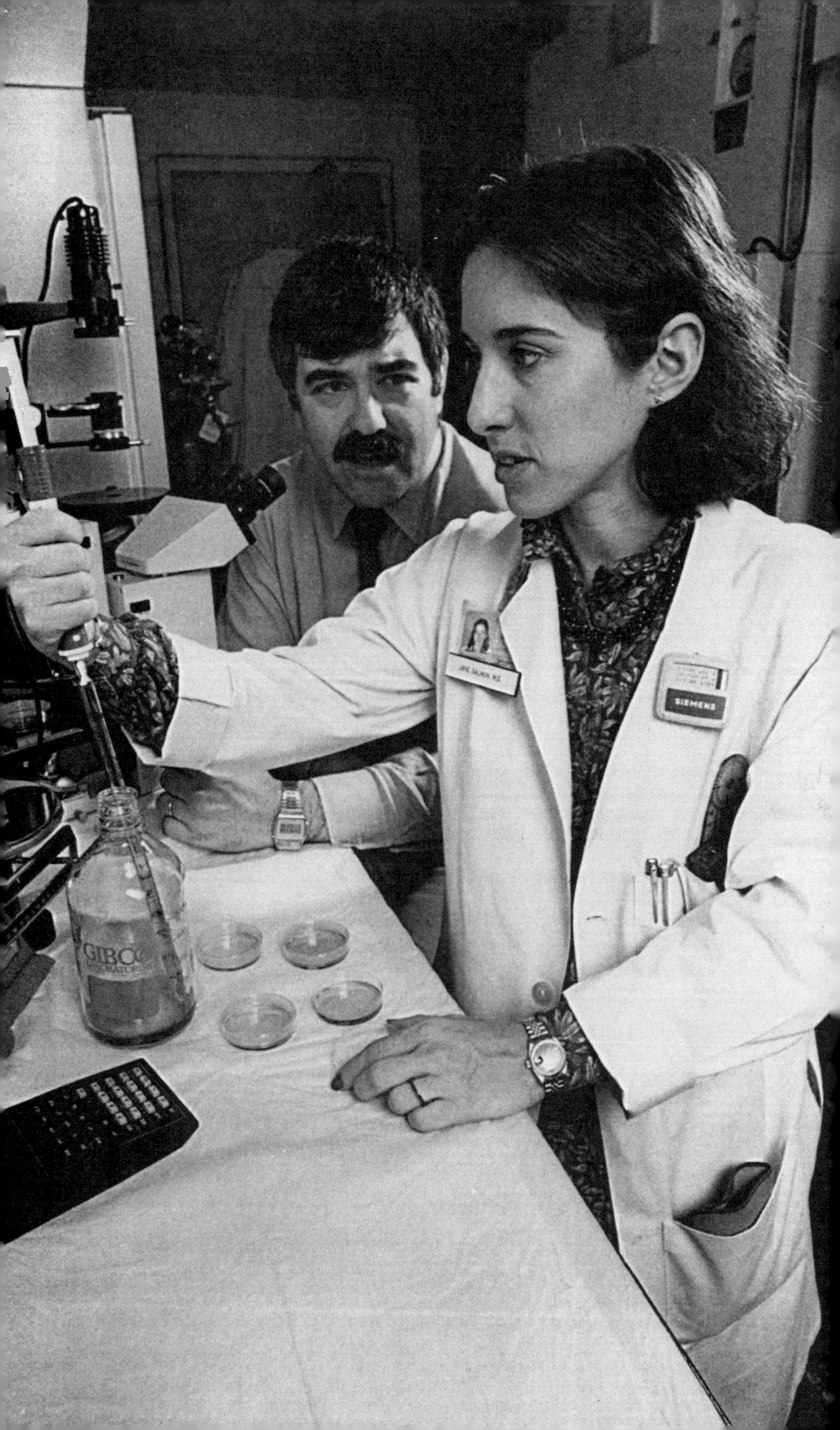
SIEMENS
GIBCO

day be able to remove that gene from a person's body and change it chemically to make it correct. The altered gene can then be replaced into the body, where it will function normally. The person who formerly had diabetes will now live a healthy and normal life.

This new knowledge raises some new ethical questions. First, should this kind of research be done on humans? On other animals? On plants? On microorganisms like bacteria? Are there some instances in which genetic engineering is ethically correct and others in which it is not?

Second, if genetic engineering *is* done on microorganisms and plants, should those altered organisms be released into nature?

THE RELEASE OF ALTERED ORGANISMS INTO NATURE

Dr. Groth's dilemma illustrates one of these problems. Now that he has found a way to produce plastic-eating bacteria, should those microorganisms be transferred out of the laboratory and into an actual waste disposal site?

Dr. Groth can think of a number of reasons *for* going ahead with the experiment. First, the experiment will have important value to science itself. No one can be sure about the results of his experiment until the bacterium is actually tested in the field. Dr. Groth feels that he has an ethical obligation to his profession to obtain and report the results of his experiment as fully and accurately as possible.

These researchers at the Orthopedic Hospital for Special Surgery in New York City are studying genetic influences on susceptibility to rheumatic disease.

Second, a successful test of the bacterium would be a great economic benefit to the nation. Communities currently spend billions of dollars on the disposal of solid wastes. Especially troublesome are plastics, which just never "go away" in nature. Dr. Groth's bacterium might solve this problem.

Third, Dr. Groth has read everything he can about the *probable* effects of releasing the altered bacterium into nature, and can find no reason to expect that it will cause harm to any other organism. Altered forms of *E. coli* already occur in nature and appear not to have caused any problems for plants, animals, or humans.

Fourth, Dr. Groth has followed all the legal requirements governing an experiment of this kind. He has studied the potential impact of his experiment on areas surrounding the waste disposal site and has received approval from the Environmental Protection Agency and from the University's Committee on Ethical Research.

Finally, Dr. Groth realizes how important this experiment can be to him personally and professionally. His work represents a real breakthrough in biochemistry and, if tested and successful, would earn him the admiration of other scientists for a solution to an important societal problem.

OPPOSITION TO THE RELEASE OF ALTERED ORGANISMS

Dr. Groth is aware of arguments against his planned experiment, however. Some critics believe that he has not tested the altered organism adequately in the laboratory. This objection presents a difficult choice because it is often hard to tell how much testing in the laboratory is "enough." Competent scientists may disagree about the number of tests needed in any one research project. Thus, Dr. Groth has to ask himself if he's acting responsibly by beginning his experiments in nature at this point.

Second, some people worry about the potential danger of the altered bacterium to plants, animals, and humans in the community. They are personally *not* convinced by Dr. Groth's studies or by those of earlier scientists. After all, this experiment is one of the first of its kind in which a genetically altered organism is released to the natural world. Whatever information scientists do have about this phenomenon, critics argue, may simply be insufficient to predict what will happen in this experiment. The risk to the health and lives of other organisms is just too great, these people say, to go ahead with the project.

Finally, some individuals object to the experiment on philosophical grounds. They believe that scientists should draw a line somewhere in their research. Some topics should simply be considered to be "off limits" to research. Genetic engineering may be one of these. Perhaps humans do not have the right to start changing the genetic structure of organisms, these critics suggest.

Probably the most outspoken critic of genetic engineering today is Jeremy Rifkin. Rifkin is not himself a scientist, but he has written and spoken extensively about the ethical issues in genetic engineering. In a case similar to that of Dr. Groth's, Rifkin has brought suit to prevent the testing of genetically altered organisms in the environment. He has written:

You and I were led to believe that with technology, if it can be done, it will be done. If there are problems, future generations will figure out a technological solution. Well, some things shouldn't be done. I don't believe human beings were made to exert all forms of power just because we can. We can split the atom, but should we have? The scientists who developed this technology said we learned something extraordinary about human life by splitting the atom. I don't think we learned a darned thing new about ourselves from splitting the atom.[12]

CHANGING HUMAN GENES

The same technology used to alter genes in bacteria can be used on human genes. The question is, *should* they? Should scientists make chemical changes in human genes in order to cure certain diseases, provide immunity against other diseases, or solve other medical problems?

The application of genetic engineering to problems of this kind is known as *human gene therapy* (HGT). The objective of HGT is to find defective human genes that cause certain diseases. Then scientists hope and expect to find ways to correct those genes in order to cure those diseases.

An example of this kind of research is the work now being done on Lesch-Nyhan disease (LND). LND results when a single gene in a boy's body (the condition affects only males) fails to function properly. This one defective gene causes a whole range of medical problems: kidneys that malfunction, arthritis, mental retardation, and a strange and uncontrollable desire to mutilate oneself, for example. LND patients often have to be tied down to prevent them from biting their fingers and lips and banging their heads against the wall. Patients with LND presently do not live beyond their teen years.

Many biologists predict that LND will be the first disease cured by human gene therapy. In fact, by the time you read this, the first successful treatment may already have occurred.

Still, the use of HGT presents ethical choices. On the one hand, the relief that HGT can bring LND patients and their families is clear. Boys whose lives would otherwise be short and filled with agony would have the opportunity of living relatively normal lives instead. The economic benefits are obvious also. Millions of dollars now spent on the care of LND patients would be available for other medical treatment and research.

Some scientists and laypersons, however, disagree

It's not nice to fool Mother Nature!

with the use of HGT. One objection reflects the view of some people that humans are special in the grand system of creation. Some religions teach, for example, that humans are higher than the animals and "a little lower than the angels." Trying to change the God-given genetic makeup of humans is, according to this argument, an act of sacrilege.

Critics worry particularly about research on *germ cells* (sperms and eggs). Changes made in these cells are transmitted from one generation to the next. They become part of the hereditary characteristics an individual passes on to his or her descendants. Changes in body cells other than germ cells (*somatic cells*) is less controversial, but still troublesome to some individuals.

Jeremy Rifkin has said, for example, that he opposes *all* forms of HGT, including techniques that would cure even the worst of human diseases. In 1984, he convinced sixty prominent religious leaders in the United States to sign a petition asking the U.S. Congress to ban all genetic engineering involving human reproductive cells.[13] Most signers later withdrew their objections to HGT on somatic cells, but continued to question research on germ cells.

A second argument against HGT is that once we start doing this kind of research, we may not know where to stop. Scientists who favor the use of HGT to treat LND may do so because of the medical relief it can bring patients. Does the same argument apply to individuals who have cystic fibrosis, muscular dystrophy, Down's syndrome, or diabetes?

What about people who are "too short"? Some children are born without a gene for making a chemical called human growth hormone (HGH). Without HGH, these children do not grow normally. They seldom grow to more than 4 feet (1.2 meters) in height. Human gene therapy could provide these people with HGH and allow them to grow normally. Are scientists justified in using HGT in this situation?

Or what about people who do have HGH, but are shorter than average? At what point does shortness become a "disease," a "disorder," a "handicap"? If you think it's proper to use HGT to treat dwarfism, is it also proper to use the technique on people who just want to be taller?

Proponents of HGT thus face another ethical dilemma. Should the procedure be used only for the treatment of diseases (such as Lesch-Nyhan disease) or for cosmetic purposes, such as making people taller (or shorter), heavier (or lighter), more intelligent (or less intelligent), or more attractive (or less attractive).

Once scientists open the door to HGT, critics say, any and all of these changes become technically possible. But are they all equally *ethical*?

For Jeremy Rifkin and some of his supporters, the answer is clear: no human gene therapy of any kind. For many scientists, the issue is more complex and a yes or no for HGT depends on the special circumstances in each case.

5

MILITARY RESEARCH

DR. SURCUT'S DILEMMA

Dr. Stan Surcut feels that he has reached a turning point in his professional career. His present job as an electrical engineer at the Plugg Electrical Company provides him with a satisfactory income and good job security. But he's gone about as far as he can go in the company. He is beginning to realize that he is stuck in his present job for the rest of his professional life.

Yet, Dr. Surcut has enough of the curiosity, ambition, and interest in research to want more from his occupation. He still thrills at the thought of breaking new ground in electrical engineering, finding new ways of doing things, making discoveries that will really change the world.

For this reason, the job opening at the U.S. Army Booming Hills Ordnance Laboratory is very appealing to Dr. Surcut. The pay wouldn't be much better than he's getting now. But he thinks he can work his way through the Department of Defense (DOD) scientific establishment quite easily.

Most important to Dr. Surcut would be the chance to work on the Army's new Strategic Army Defense System

(SADS). He knows that some of the most exciting research anywhere in the world in the field of telecommunications is going on under SADS' auspices. The SADS job looks like just the chance he's been waiting for.

However, Dr. Surcut's conscience has begun to trouble him about this opportunity. He knows that, despite its name, SADS is an offensive as well as a defensive weapons system. Once SADS is fully developed, his nation will have the ability to launch a nuclear attack on any other nation in the world with a good chance of destroying that nation before it can respond.

The question troubling Dr. Surcut is whether he should devote his intelligence and talents to the construction of such a terrible weapons system. Were his country at war, the decision would be easier. He would certainly do everything he could to prevent the conquest of his homeland by another nation. But the world is at peace. Is he still justified in spending the rest of his life working on tools of death and destruction?

Dr. Surcut's wife thinks his choice is clear. "If you don't do the job, Stan," she has said, "some other scientist will. And that other scientist might not be a God-fearing religious man, as you are. At least you can bring some feeling for morality to the job. Say yes, Stan."

Dr. Surcut's older brother disagrees. "Just because you *do* care about morality," he argues, "you *must* draw a line somewhere. You know that the things you invent will never have any practical use except to destroy life and property. This is your opportunity to put into practice the highest ideals you believe in. Say no, Stan."

SCIENCE AND WEAPONS RESEARCH THROUGH HISTORY

Scientists have been doing military research for centuries. Some of the earliest stories about scientific research, in fact, tell about the invention of new military weapons. Historians report, for example, how the ancient Greek scientist Archimedes almost singlehandedly defeated the forces of Rome in the second century B.C. He is said to have designed giant lenses that concentrated the sun's rays on the enemy's fleet, setting its ships on fire. And he is supposed to have invented enormous cranes that could lift enemy ships out of the water.

Throughout most of history, scientists appear to have had little ethical choice about taking part in their nation's war efforts. The inventor of the automatic rifle may have been troubled about the men and women who would be killed by his invention. But the loss of those lives had to be balanced against the survival of one's own homeland.

From this perspective, saving a nation was far more important than saving a few individual lives. Developing the automatic rifle, a weapon of death and destruction, could thus be justified as an ethically correct choice.

The same argument could be employed in most wars. When a nation's very existence hangs in the balance, a scientist's participation in weapons research is relatively easy to defend as the right thing to do.

World War II presented scientists with a new dilemma, however. The atomic bomb, developed toward the end of the war, was not just another weapon. The bomb could be used not just to kill a few thousand or even a few million humans; the new weapon threatened the very existence of the human race itself. The new dilemma for scientists became one that involved a choice between the survival of a nation and the survival of the human species.

The ethical questions of weapons research have certainly not become any simpler in the last forty years. The destructive potential of new weapons systems becomes

Nuclear test in Nevada, 1957

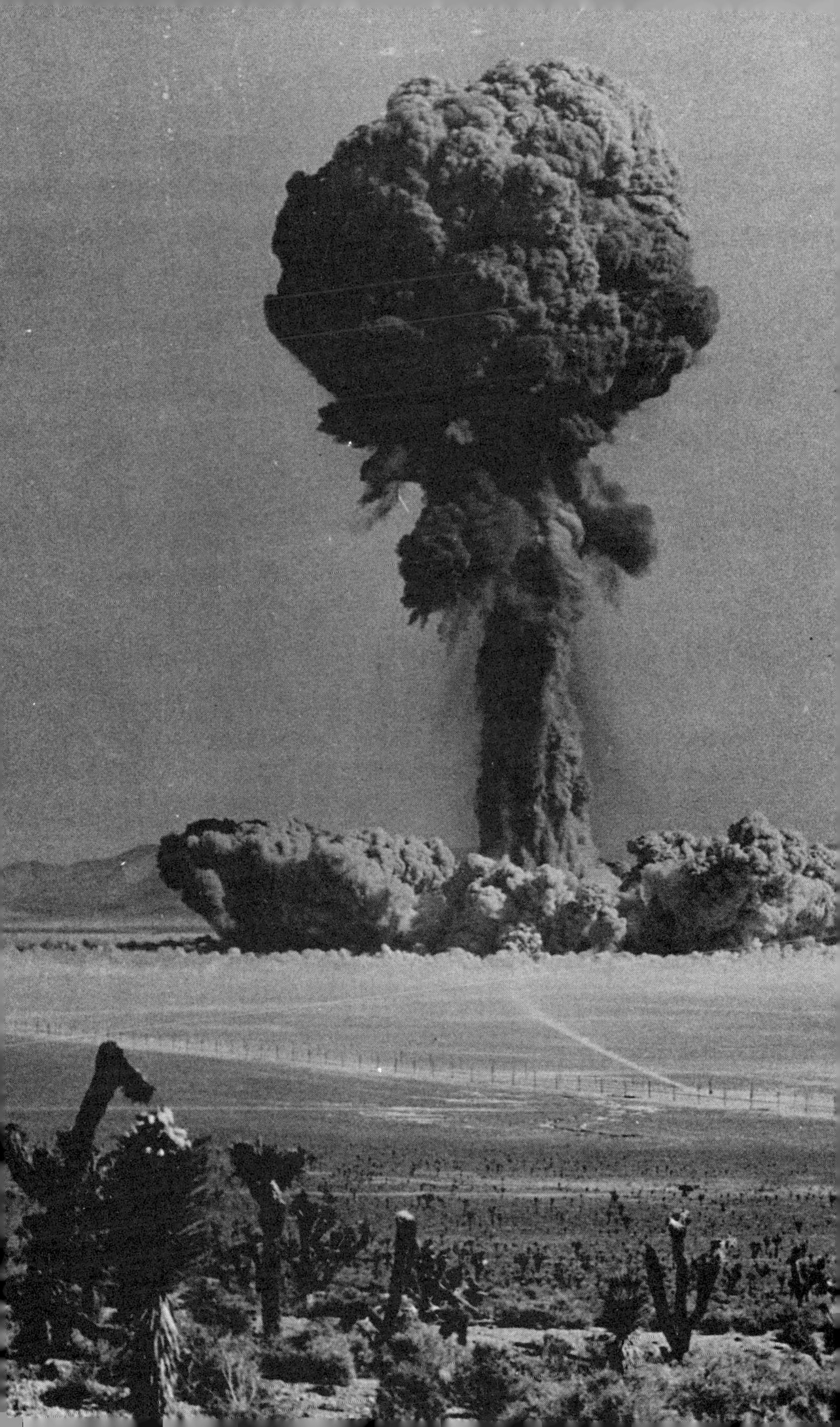

"All we want is something new that will incapacitate the enemy without giving us bad press."

greater with each decade. And the nations who are developing these systems are *not* at war. In this setting, what arguments must scientists like Dr. Surcut consider *for* and *against* their participation in weapons research?

"I CHOOSE TO WORK ON WEAPONS RESEARCH BECAUSE . . ."

For many scientists, the ethical issue about military research has really not changed at all. Although better weapons are not needed to win a war right now, they *are* needed to *prevent* a war, that is, to guarantee peace. In this sense, scientists who help with the development of new weapons systems are doing their patriotic duty. Their choice is an ethically correct one.

Indeed, one might argue that the right thing to do is to never stop looking for more destructive, more powerful weapons. The more terrible these weapons become, this argument goes, the less likely it is they will ever be used. As the destructive potential of weapons grows, nations will be ever less and less willing to start an armed conflict. "We design and build weapons," one researcher has said, "in order that they may never be used."

A second reason for choosing to work on military weapons is the ethical obligation scientists feel to their own profession. Most scientists believe that their primary professional responsibility is to learn about the natural world, to make discoveries and inventions. The purposes to which these discoveries and inventions are put by society may not always be happy ones. But those are the ethical choices nonscientists have to make.

For many scientists, *gaining* knowledge about the physical world and *using* that knowledge are two separate issues. A scientist has an ethical obligation to do his or her job in the most conscientious and responsible way possible. Questions about the application of scientific knowl-

"It's a personalized A-bomb, gentlemen, designed to exterminate our selected victims with no unnecessary loss of life."

edge can just not be answered by scientists, many researchers would argue.

"I CHOOSE NOT TO WORK ON WEAPONS RESEARCH BECAUSE . . ."

For each of the arguments used to justify military research, scientists can find an opposing position. The notion that new and better weapons are simply too terrible to be used, for example, seems absurd to many people. Can we find *any* example from history in which governments rejected a weapons system because it was too effective, too destructive, too frightening?

The reality is, some scientists believe, that the fact that weapons are being developed guarantees they *will* be used. We may hope and plan to put off that awful moment when some new weapons system is actually deployed. But rest assured, these observers insist, that moment *will* come.

The patriotic and ethical decision for scientists, then, is to see that those weapons are never developed. If they are never developed, they can never be used. The ethically logical position is that national security and worldwide peace can come about only when scientists refuse to provide new and more powerful weapons.

Also, many scientists now argue that trying to draw a line between discovery and invention, on the one hand, and application, on the other, is an unrealistic, obsolete, and dangerous thing for scientists to do. That practice may have made sense a hundred years ago, when science was less intimately involved with our daily lives.

But everyone today can see how rapidly and how dramatically developments in science affect our national security, our safety, our health, and our way of life. Scientists can no longer hide behind some abstract philosophy of "value-free" scientific research as a way of doing any research that interests them without also assessing the ethical implications of that research. Like it or not, this argument says, scientists must become involved in the ethical debate over weapons research.

Finally, the question arises as to the probable success of some current weapons research. Some researchers (but certainly not all) believe that projects such as President Reagan's Strategic Defense Initiative (SDI, or "Star Wars" project) are so complex and so technically difficult that virtually no hope exists for their success.

The *ethical* question for these scientists is whether they should take part in a project with such a low probability of success. The temptations to do so are great. Exciting projects, involving large research teams and massive funding, grow out of weapons research. The enthusiasm Dr. Surcut feels for such a project is understandable.

But what if he strongly suspects that the project is unlikely ever to be successful? Is he still justified in taking government money to do research on the system?

Few topics illustrate the contrast between ethical dilemmas that scientists have faced in the past and those they face today as does the question of military research.

6

WHEN SCIENTISTS SPEAK OUT

DR. KARNIEWSKI'S DILEMMA

Dr. Agnes Karniewski is troubled by an advertisement she saw last evening on television. The ad told about a new fuel additive "guaranteed to improve gas mileage in any car by at least 10 percent." Dr. Karniewski's concern is based on the fact that she was involved in the testing of that additive.

Her employer, Northwest Testing Labs, received a contract to field-test Additive X160 from its inventor, AddCo, more than a year ago. Dr. Karniewski was one of five researchers assigned to verify AddCo's claims that X160 would "significantly increase gas mileage during normal driving."

Dr. Karniewski's team failed to confirm this claim. Cars running on gas to which X160 had been added got essentially the same gas mileage as cars running on gas without X160. In fact, Dr. Karniewski's studies suggested that X160 was likely to cause minor engine damage in some cars.

Dr. Karniewski reported the results of her team's research to Dr. Baird Manners, director of research at Northwest, nearly six months ago. Her work on the project completed, she assumed that AddCo would drop the X160 project or would attempt to improve the additive. She did *not* expect to see the product being advertised as something she knew it wasn't.

For Dr. Karniewski, the appearance of the X160 ad on television presents a clear moral dilemma. What should she say or do about this apparently false advertising? What ethical responsibility does she have, if any, to see that AddCo does not continue presenting information to the public which she believes is not true?

On the one hand, she is upset that the company is using lies (or so she is convinced) to sell its products. People who buy and use X160 will be throwing away their money on a useless product and may even damage their car's engine in the process.

But Dr. Karniewski's decision is not a simple one. She knows what Dr. Manners's position is likely to be. From previous discussions, she knows that Dr. Manners wants to avoid controversies concerning the products they test. Northwest's job, he insists, is to conduct careful, thorough, objective research on products sent to them. Once the results of that research have been reported to the product manufacturer, Northwest's job is done. Period. Going any further than that, Dr. Manners argues, is professionally irresponsible and may well open a Pandora's box of controversy. Dr. Karniewski is not sure she wants to become involved in this kind of controversy.

Having considered Dr. Manners's position, Dr. Karniewski still wonders if she has an ethical responsibility to do something about AddCo's advertising campaign for X160. The problem is that she doesn't know what, if anything, to do.

WHEN ETHICAL CHOICES CALL FOR ACTION

You may have considered some of the possible courses of action that would have occurred to Dr. Karniewski and other scientists; namely, she could:

"On the other hand, my responsibility to society makes me want to stop right here."

- Do nothing at all
- Bring her concerns and the data she collected to Dr. Manners
- Express her concerns to a public agency such as the Federal Trade Commission or some consumer action group
- Carry her case to the public in newspaper articles, radio and television interviews, and public addresses
- Enlist the cooperation of other scientists who might be interested in this issue or in related issues
- Resign her job as an act of protest and follow up with any or all of the above actions.

The first decision Dr. Karniewski has to make is whether to do anything at all. Should she find some way of protesting AddCo's ad campaign, or should she simply accept their actions and Dr. Manners's decision?

This dilemma might not be so difficult if she had only herself to think about. She could determine what seemed right or wrong according to her own conscience and act on that decision.

But ethical dilemmas are seldom that simple. Scientists such as Dr. Karniewski have to consider how their actions will affect the company for which they work, the scientific profession, of which they are a member, and society at large. In deciding what to do, they will have to weigh the expectations of all these institutions against each other.

To make things even more difficult, each of these institutions may have *contrasting* ethical expectations. For example, Dr. Karniewski realizes that respect for truth is one of the highest of all priorities in science. To allow the

Time to blow the whistle

release of information that she knows (or believes) to be incorrect probably seems clearly unethical to her as it might to any other scientist. Thus, she may feel compelled to act to *prevent* AddCo from stating false information about X160.

But the scientific community also values the process of replication. "Truth" in science is what has been tested and verified by many individuals. What may be important in the case of X160 is not Dr. Karniewski's own research but the cumulative result of many experiments. In this sense, she may be wrong in insisting that her results provide the final, correct assessment of this product.

The company for which Dr. Karniewski works also has varying ethical expectations. On the one hand, Northwest almost certainly expects that Dr. Karniewski will do her job thoroughly and accurately. Does that mean that, in the case of X160, she should push aggressively for *her* view of the research? Perhaps the company wants and expects that she will continue to fight for what she believes is right, even if it means "going over the head" of her supervisor.

On the other hand, the company probably places a high priority on loyalty. It may feel that an employee should

J. Robert Oppenheimer, the brilliant physicist who directed the project that led to the development of the first atomic bomb, was outspoken and, perhaps, naive. The government suspended his security clearance, he fell into permanent disgrace, and his life was never again the same.

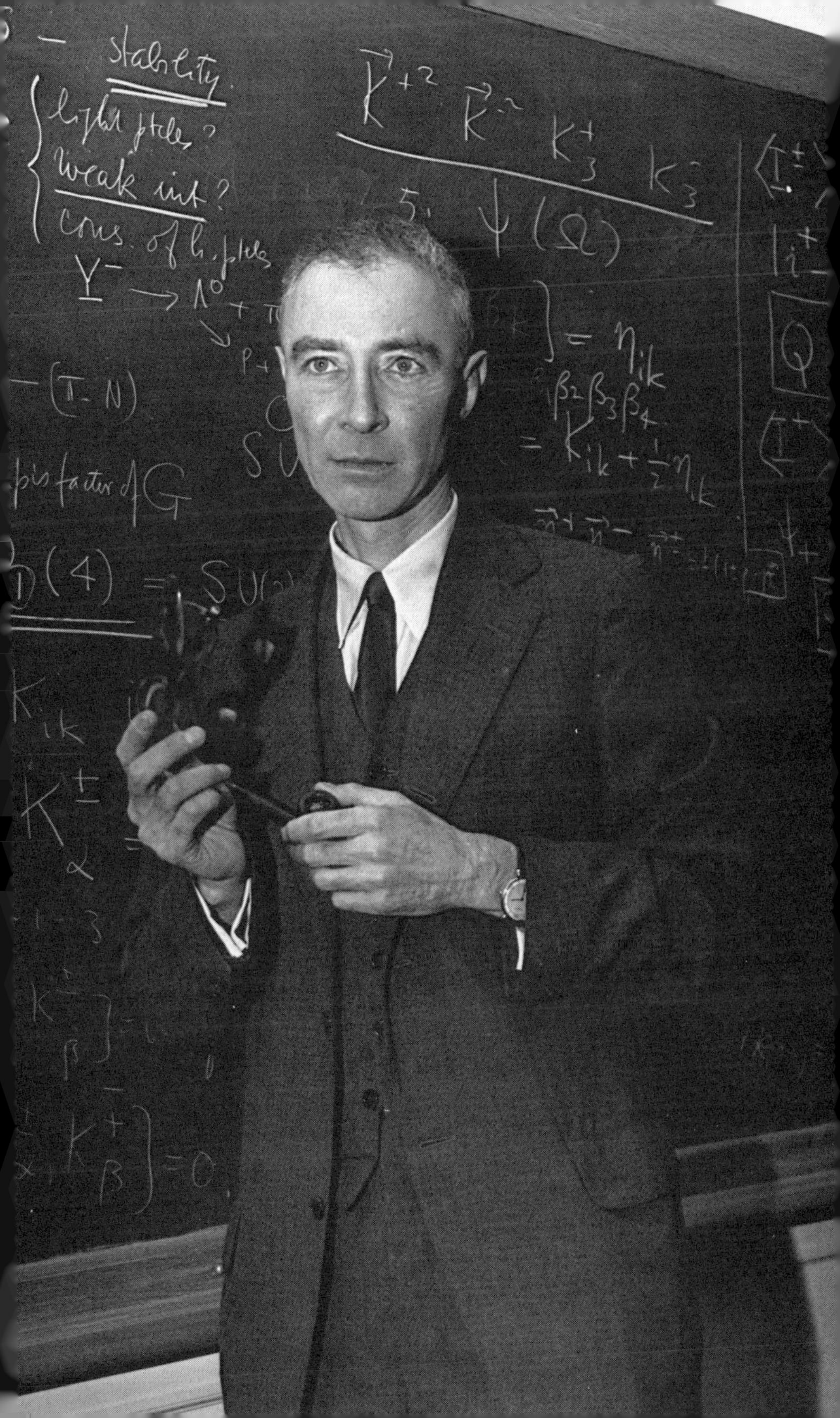
stability
weak int ?

observe the "chain of command" and recognize that Dr. Manners may know more or have better judgment than the indiviudal employee.

The ethical demands of society at large can be in conflict also. Dr. Karniewski may believe that her fellow citizens count on her for accurate information about new products. Their health, safety and very lives often depend on the research results that come out of her lab. So how can it be right for her to sit by and let AddCo disseminate information which she believes to be false?

But society may not necessarily want Dr. Karniewski to argue her case in public. In most states, the courts have said that government agencies and private companies have the right to decide whom they do and do not want working for them. An employee who is dissatisfied with an employer's decisions is usually expected to resolve those disagreements within the organization, to say nothing about his or her objections, or to leave the organization. However, some states now have laws protecting such employees, and some scientific and technical societies have committees to help scientists decide what to do when faced with such problems.

Finally, Dr. Karniewski has to listen to what her own conscience has to say about this situation. Again, she may hear differing messages. On the one hand, she might believe strongly in her responsibility to truth in science, as she sees it. On the other hand, she may place great value on loyalty to those for whom she works. If these two values are in conflict, the question may become which is "more right" than the other.

In the end, factors having nothing at all to do with ethics may influence Dr. Karniewski's decision, even if that decision is essentially an ethical choice. For example, perhaps she just doesn't want to lose her job at Northwest. After weighing all the arguments outlined above, she may finally decide that keeping her position at the testing laboratory is simply more important than all the rights and wrongs involved.

CHOICES OF ACTION

Suppose that Dr. Karniewski decides she has to do *something* about the AddCo ad campaign. What should that "something" be?

Dr. Karniewski's predicament is not at all uncommon in science today. A person sees what he or she believes to be shoddy experimentation, fraud, attempts at cover-ups, biased research, deceptive reports, or some other behavior that appears to be unethical. The observer fails to persuade a supervisor or company or agency to act on his or her report and decides to take the case to the general public. Anyone who "goes public" in a situation like this is sometimes called a *whistle-blower.*

Choosing to "blow the whistle" on an individual, a company, or a government agency can be a risky act. The whistle-blower may be (1) demoted, transferred, or fired, (2) labeled publicly as a troublemaker, (3) harassed at home and on the job, and/or (4) threatened with professional disgrace.

Whistle-blowers cannot expect much assistance from the law either. Only two states, Michigan and Connecticut, have laws designed to protect employees, in both public and private occupations, who expose illegal or dangerous employer activities. The federal government and a number of state governments have enacted legislation of this kind covering government employees, but not workers in private industry.

No one is yet certain how effectively laws such as these will protect prospective whistle-blowers. For someone who sees actions that seem to be immoral or illegal, then, the choice can be an agonizing one. Shall I act according to my conscience, or should I do what my employers want me to do? Or how can I persuade my employer to act responsibly?

THE CHALLENGER DISASTER: WHAT ARE THE LESSONS?

Modern technology is often very complex. That complexity can create difficult choices, both technical and ethical, for scientists. The space shuttle *Challenger* disaster of January 28, 1986, illustrates that point.

Challenger exploded and was destroyed only seventy-three seconds after liftoff from Cape Canaveral. The cause of the disaster, in which all seven astronauts were killed, appears to have been a faulty O-ring gasket on one of the booster rockets. Scientists and the general public asked how such a terrible accident could have occurred.

During the Presidential Commission's investigation of the accident, some interesting points came to light. First, engineers had known for more than three years that the O-ring gaskets were a potential source of trouble in the shuttle. Yet research on a revised gasket had been postponed for financial reasons for two years.[14]

Investigators also learned that some engineers at Morton Thiokol, manufacturer of the gasket and of the booster itself, had recommended on the night before the scheduled launch that the launch be postponed.[15] They argued that the company could not predict how the questionable gaskets would perform in the abnormally cold temperatures expected at the launch pad the next day.

Both engineers and NASA officials found themselves facing a difficult decision at that point. On the one hand, no one could really be sure what might happen during the launch or even whether the shuttle was in any danger at all. The Morton Thiokol engineers apparently felt enough doubt to recommend against launch, however.

On the other hand, NASA officials had no concrete data to show that the gasket would fail. They were also feeling a great deal of pressure to stay on their planned shuttle launch schedule. In recent years, NASA had apparently been working very hard to prove that the shuttle could be an economic success. And that meant staying with a schedule of twenty-four launches a year.

One NASA budget analyst noted that "it was my understanding that urgency to meet the scheduled shuttle flight rate was the primary motivation for not suspending flights while . . . repairs were made."[16]

For whatever reason, NASA officials appear to have exerted considerable pressure on Morton Thiokol engineers to approve the scheduled launch, which they ultimately did.

Analyzing this issue in retrospect is fairly easy. Given all the engineers knew about problems with the O-ring gasket, perhaps the launch should have been delayed. But, in fact, NASA had issued seven hundred forty "redundancy waivers," statements allowing the use of shuttle parts whose safety and effectiveness had been questioned by engineers. How would anyone have know which of these seven hundred forty possible trouble spots to be most concerned about in this launch?

What choices did the Morton Thiokol engineers really have in this situation? Should they have insisted that the launch be delayed? They had not only lack of data to worry about, but also the realization that NASA had just recently invited other engineering firms to bid on the kind of shuttle work that Morton Thiokol was currently doing. Still, at some point, the experts in the case (the Morton Thiokol engineers) must have felt strongly enough to recommend a "no-go" decision on the launch.

The risks Morton Thiokol engineers took in "rocking the boat" with NASA's launch schedule became obvious as the Presidential Commission finished its investigation of the accident. The Morton Thiokol engineer who argued strongly against the scheduled launch was reassigned to a new position with apparently no responsibilities within the company.[17] Both he and the Commission chairman viewed this assignment as punishment for his testimony before the Commission.

SOCIAL ACTION GROUPS

Dr. Karniewski's hypothetical ethical dilemma is fairly specific. Under many circumstances, it probably could be resolved within her own workplace. But scientists also develop interests in broader ethical issues, such as the use of nuclear weapons. In such cases, they may band together to form associations to work on an issue of common interest. One such group is the Union of Concerned Scientists; a publication that reflects broad issues is *The Bulletin of the Atomic Scientists.*

The Union of Concerned Scientists (UCS) originated as an informal group of teachers and students at the Massachusetts Institute of Technology. The common issue which united the group was concern about the participation of scientists in the Vietnam War. The group recognized that large numbers of scientists were contributing, often with considerable enthusiasm, to the development of new weapons systems for use in Vietnam.

Members of the UCS created the association in order to examine ethical issues raised by the role of scientists in the war. Since its early days, the Union has expanded its interests to include the use of nuclear power plants, arms control, and space-based weapons systems ("Star Wars").

In all its campaigns, UCS makes use of a wide variety of educational and lobbying techniques. The Union has produced documentary videotapes, published at least four major books, sponsored nationwide "teach-ins" at more than five hundred colleges and universities, commissioned research studies, and released a number of "briefing papers" on nuclear and energy issues.

In addition, the Union maintains a speaker's bureau,

arranges for and assists with lobbying, works with other interested groups of scientists, and coordinates letter-writing and other campaigns aimed at influencing legislation.

A somewhat different way of dealing with ethical questions is a scientific journal, *The Bulletin of the Atomic Scientists.* The *Bulletin* began in 1945 as a newsletter published by and for scientists working on the first atomic bomb. These workers saw the *Bulletin* as a mechanism by which they could exchange ideas about the social and ethical consequences of their work.

Over the years, the *Bulletin* has grown to become one of the most highly respected journals on nuclear issues in the world. Today, it appears as a monthly publication of forty to sixty-four pages. Its focus is still largely on nuclear issues. Each year, questions about every aspect of nuclear science—nuclear power production, nuclear weapons, medical uses of radioactive isotopes, and radioactive waste disposal, for example—are debated by top authorities in each field.

In addition, however, the editors have expanded the scope of the *Bulletin* to include other topics, such as chemical and biological warfare, space research, and environmental issues.

Like the Union of Concerned Scientists, the *Bulletin* provides a mechanism by which scientists can express their social and ethical concerns on science-related issues.

WHEN IS AN "EXPERT" NOT AN EXPERT?

The issue troubling Dr. Karniewski is one that arises as a result of her expertise in a particular field of science. Because of her training and experience in and knowledge of the chemistry of fuel additives, she probably has a legitimate reason to worry about the use of X160.

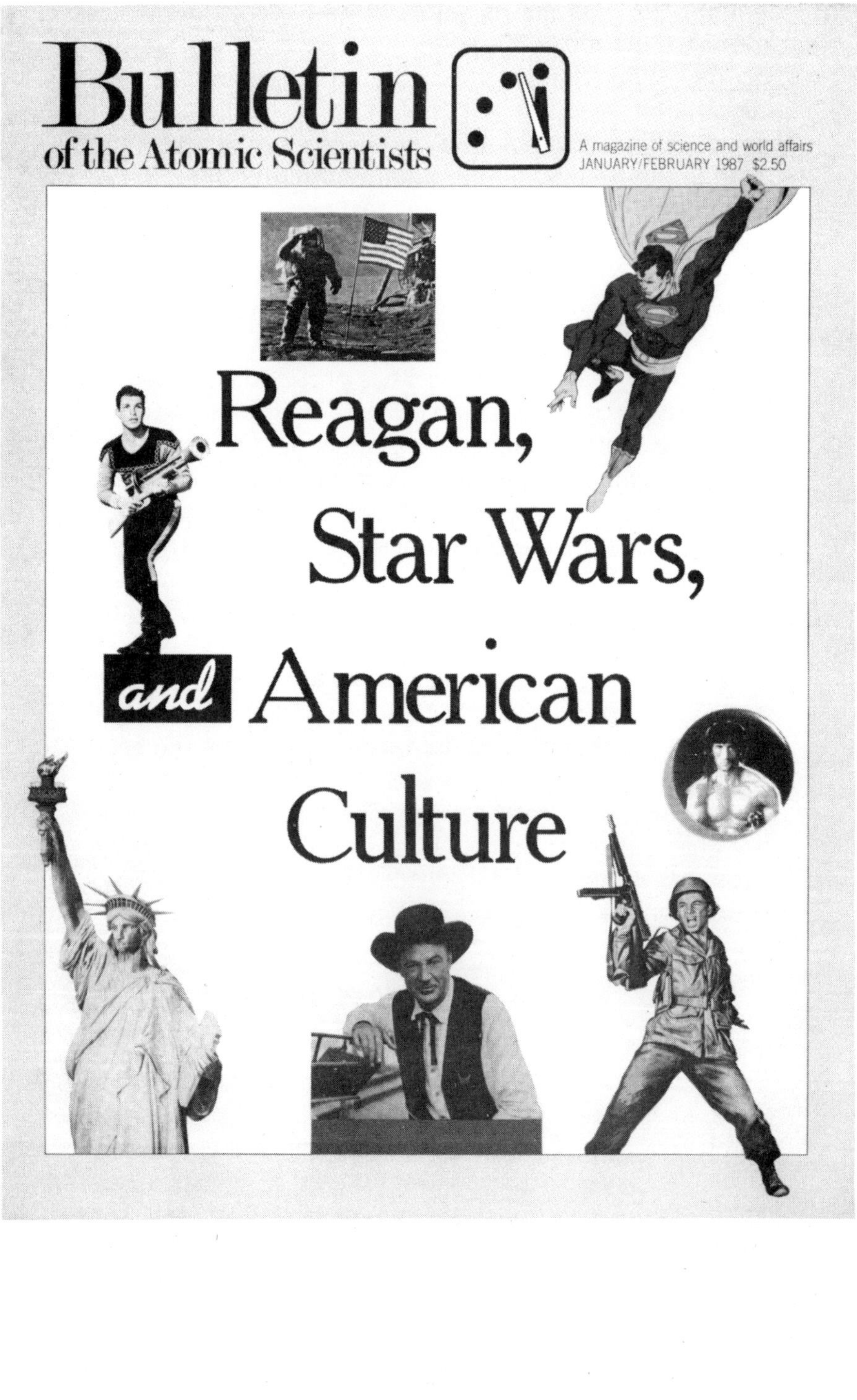

Bulletin
of the Atomic Scientists

A magazine of science and world affairs
JANUARY/FEBRUARY 1987 $2.50

Reagan, Star Wars, *and* American Culture

In other instances, scientists become involved in ethical debates *outside* their field of expertise. For example, suppose that Dr. Karniewski had particularly strong feelings about the question of legalized abortion. Nothing in her professional experience would qualify her as an "expert" on this topic.

Still, she may have such strong feelings on the subject that she feels an ethical obligation to make her views known. In this case, the arguments for and against her speaking out and the ways in which she might express her opinions are somewhat different from her choices in the X160 case.

To begin with, no one in this country is likely to question Dr. Karniewski's *constitutional right* to speak out on legalized abortion, X160, or any other subject. The First Amendment guarantees that right to all citizens of the United States. So, like any other citizen, Dr. Karniewski can write letters to the newspapers, address public gatherings, take part in special-interest groups, appear before governmental bodies, and take part in that whole range of activities by which all citizens can express their views on public questions.

The question is what, if anything, does Dr. Karniewski's expertise in chemistry have to do with her statements and actions on the issue of abortion?

Some scientists have argued that their opinions on problems outside their field of expertise deserve special consideration because of their background and experience in science. Their training and work helps them, they say, to develop an objective, logical, and rational method of solving problems that nonscientists are less likely to

The Bulletin of the Atomic Scientists
*is one of the most highly respected
journals on nuclear issues in the world.*

use. The respected scientists and author C. P. Snow once said that "The scientists that I have known . . . have been in certain respects just perceptibly more morally admirable than most other groups of intelligent men."

Perhaps you have heard someone recommend "the scientific method" as a way of solving everyday problems, from buying a car to choosing a wife or husband. Thus, when some scientists express an opinion on social policy, politics, economics, or morality, they may expect to have their ideas receive special weight. Is this an ethically sound position?

People outside the field of science sometimes seem to agree with this philosophy. Would *your* response be any different to a lecture presented by *Dr.* Karniewski versus one given by *Ms.* Karniewski? Some of us are impressed immediately by the initials Ph.D. or M.D. after a person's name even if we know little else about that person. That scientist's expertise in botany or astronomy or geology can just seem to transfer to anything he or she has to say on *any* topic.

For that scientist, the temptation to take advantage of that "automatic respect" may be great. If Dr. Karniewski knows that the public admires her *just because* she has a Ph.D. and is an "expert," does she have the right to *use* that respect when she speaks out on another subject, such as abortion?

Scientists have done just that on many occasions in the past. For example, during the Vietnam War, groups of scientists sometimes purchased full-page advertisements in newspapers, asking the president to escalate or to end the war.

The signers of these petitions sometimes added their academic titles (*Dr.* Smart or Robert Wiley, *Professor of Botany*) to their names. What purpose did this action serve? The scientists apparently felt that identifying themselves as a "scientist" or a "scholar" might add weight to the position offered. The implication is that the opinion of

Dr. Thomas Jones on warfare is more worthy than that of *Mr.* Thomas Jones. If the issue is important enough, even the most conscientious scientists may want to take advantage of this small additional recognition society has given them.

Perhaps the best-known and most controversial example of a scientist's speaking outside his field of expertise is Dr. William B. Shockley. Dr. Shockley received a Nobel Prize in 1956 for his role in the invention of the transistor. He is universally acknowledged and respected as an expert in the field of physics.

But Dr. Shockley has long been interested in another topic *outside* of the field of physics, namely, the origin of human intelligence and the relationship of intelligence to race. Although Dr. Shockley has no formal training in psychology, he has read extensively on the subject. He has become convinced that intelligence, like hair and eye color, is inherited, and that blacks in the United States are genetically less intelligent than whites. For many years, Dr. Shockley has been presenting these ideas in books, articles, and public addresses.[18]

Do Dr. Shockley's background and experience in physics lend credence to his ideas in a field in which he is not a trained expert? When he announces a lecture on race and intelligence, should he mention that he is a Nobel laureate? Should he expect that his readers and listeners will give his arguments the same weight as those of a professional psychologist? Are his personal beliefs about race and intelligence so strong and so important that he can use his prestige in physics to win debating points in the field of psychology?

Many of Dr. Shockley's opponents say that a scientist's knowledge, beliefs, and ideas outside his or her field of expertise are no better and no worse than those of the average citizen.[19] Whatever objectivity scientists may have in their own work does not necessarily carry over into any other part of their lives. A chemist's opinion of the best

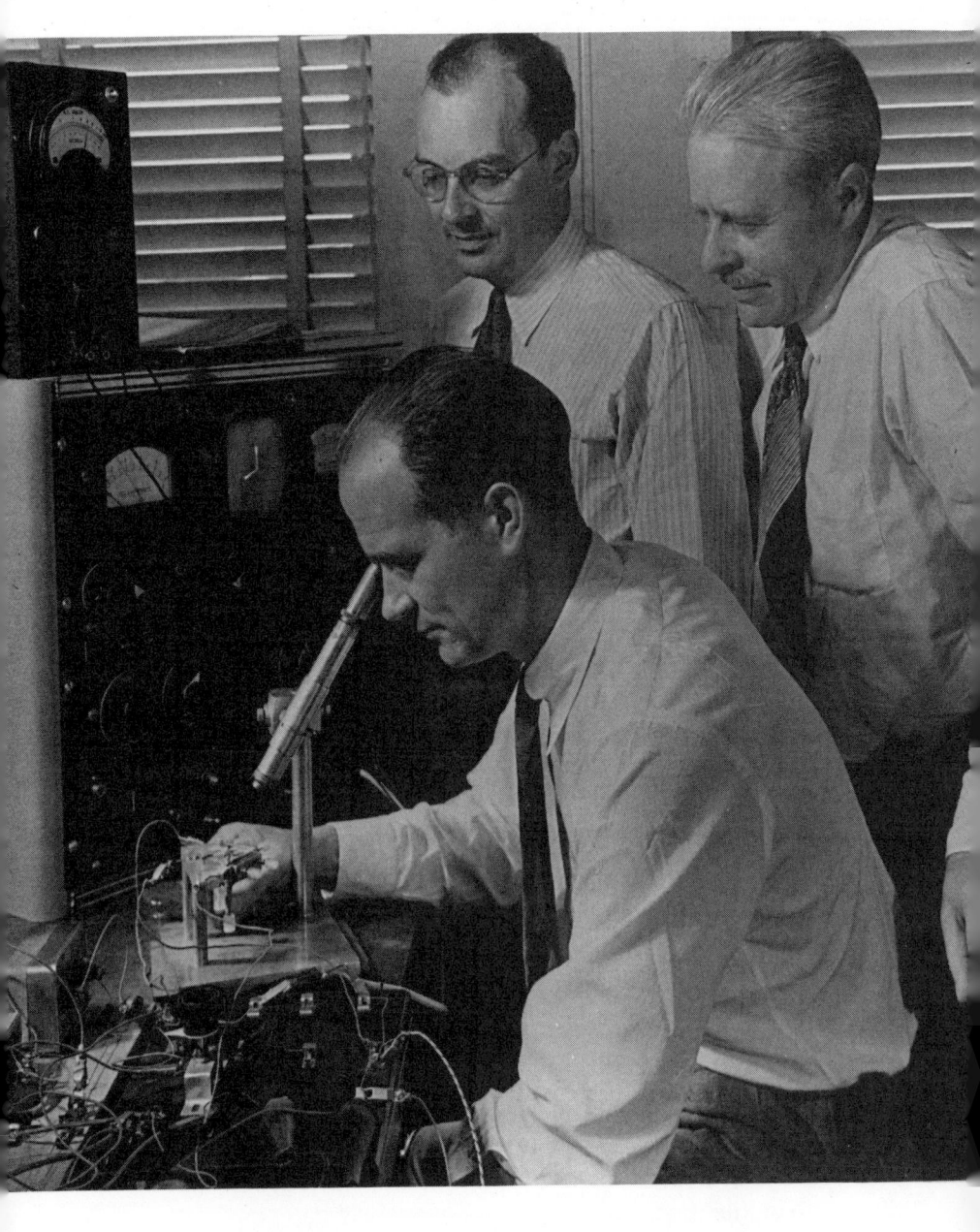

*William Shockely (seated), John Bardeen (left),
and Walter Brattain—the inventors of the transistor*

car to buy, the best person to choose for president, or the best way to have peace in the world does not deserve any more consideration than that of a house painter, a lawyer, or an airline pilot.

When scientists use their professional credentials to promote ideas outside their own field, these critics say, they are being dishonest and unethical. They are claiming special significance for ideas which really don't have or deserve such significance.

Some of the objections to Shockley's work have alleged the fact that he is really just an amateur in the field of intelligence. The members of the Department of Genetics at Shockley's own Stanford University called his work "hackneyed, pseudoscientific justification for class and race prejudice."[20] And, on one occasion, a group of Shockley's fellow scientists at the National Academy of Sciences responded to his ideas with a statement that "such simplistic notions of race, intelligence, and 'human quality' [are] unworthy of serious consideration by a body of scientists."

The issues raised by scientists speaking outside their field of expertise sometimes put them in a "Catch-22" situation, that is, damned if they do (speak out) and damned if they don't. A 1985 editorial by columnist Guy Wright illustrates this dilemma. Wright first observed that "for the physicists to dismiss [President Reagan's "Star Wars" project] as 'technically dubious' is within the scope of their expertise." That is, Mr. Wright agrees that scientists can and should advise society about technical questions.

But then he points out that scientists have no special expertise when they think and talk about political questions. He goes on to say that "calling it [the 'Star Wars' project] 'politically unwise' is per se a political judgment, which takes them outside their field."[21] With this statement, Mr. Wright suggests that the right and privilege that all Americans have to take public positions on national policy is not permitted to scientists apparently *just because* they are experts in science.

As science and technology have greater impact on our daily lives, scientists will be confronted with more opportunities to speak out in public. Whether they do so as experts in their own field or as individual citizens, they face a number of ethical choices about whether to speak out at all and, if so, the proper channels through which to express their views.

7

SCIENCE AS BIG BUSINESS

DR. CARDOZA'S DILEMMA

Dr. Rita Cardoza faces a difficult decision. As chairwoman of the Department of Biology at Uprite University, she has a secure, well-paying, respected place in her profession. Thus, the job as director of research offered her recently by the Green Leaf Tobacco Company comes as a mixed blessing.

On the one hand, Green Leaf could pay more than twice the salary Dr. Cardoza is making at Uprite. In addition, she would have virtually unlimited resources to pursue her special research interest: the relationship of skin cancer and smoking.

On the other hand, Dr. Cardoza is reasonably happy in her present position. She is not sure that she wants to give up her academic appointment to take on a new career in industry.

Probably the most agonizing consideration Dr. Cardoza faces concerns the controversy over studies showing that tobacco consumption can cause cancer. Some of Dr. Cardoza's own earlier research has been enthusiastically praised and bitterly criticized by the American Cancer

Society, the tobacco companies, the general public, and her own colleagues in cancer research.

Dr. Cardoza's position on the tobacco/cancer controversy is not much different from that of the Tobacco Institute. She knows that scientists have found a *statistical correlation* between smoking and cancer. But she also knows that the existence of this correlation does not prove that smoking *causes* cancer. Dr. Cardoza has written articles and given legislative testimony in support of this position. She suspects, in fact, that the Green Leaf offer may have come as a result of her reputation as a "pro-industry" spokesperson.

Still, her position on the question is not as firm now as it was ten years ago. And she can imagine that additional research might cause her to change her mind at some time in the future.

The problem is how much freedom to change her mind she would have at Green Leaf. The company has assured her that it wants only to discover the truth about the medical effects of tobacco use. Still, Dr. Cardoza can hardly imagine that the company would hire, pay, and provide research support to a scientist who finds evidence that smoking *causes* cancer.

Besides, Dr. Cardoza realizes that the job offered her is not just that of a working scientist. As director of research, she would be expected to represent the company at many professional and public functions. In this situation, it seems unreasonable to expect that she could present anything other than the company's position on the smoking controversy. How could she square that commitment with her personal and scientific commitment to the open-minded search for truth?

A cigarette advertisement from 1929

"Light a Lucky and you'll never miss sweets that make you fat"

Constance Talmadge,
Charming Motion
Picture Star

INSTEAD of eating between meals... instead of fattening sweets... beautiful women keep youthful slenderness these days by smoking Luckies. The smartest and loveliest women of the modern stage take this means of keeping slender... when others nibble fattening sweets, they light a Lucky!

Lucky Strike is a delightful blend of the world's finest tobaccos. These tobaccos are toasted—a costly extra process which develops and improves the flavor. That's why Luckies are a delightful alternative for fattening sweets. That's why there's real health in Lucky Strike. That's why folks say: "It's good to smoke Luckies."

For years this has been no secret to those men who keep fit and trim. They know that Luckies steady their nerves and do not harm their physical condition. They know that Lucky Strike is the favorite cigarette of many prominent athletes, who must keep in good shape. They respect the opinions of 20,679 physicians who maintain that Luckies are less irritating to the throat than other cigarettes.

A reasonable proportion of sugar in the diet is recommended, but the authorities are overwhelming that too many fattening sweets are harmful and that too many such are eaten by the American people. So, for moderation's sake we say:—

Constance Talmadge,
Charming Motion
Picture Star

"REACH FOR A LUCKY
INSTEAD OF A SWEET."

"It's toasted"

No Throat Irritation—No Cough. © 1929, The American Tobacco Co., Manufacturers

Coast to coast radio hook-up every Saturday night through the National Broadcasting Company's network. The Lucky Strike Dance Orchestra in "The Tunes that made Broadway, Broadway."

Reach for a
Lucky instead
of a sweet.

WHAT DO SCIENTISTS OWE THEIR EMPLOYERS?

Dr. Cardoza's dilemma calls attention to a side of science about which we have said little: the economics of research. Some science today is Big Business, and for many scientists, that fact creates a number of ethical problems.

For example, Dr. Cardoza will have to determine the relative degrees of her loyalty to her company and to her commitment to truth and to the scientific profession. On the one hand, Dr. Cardoza is a *scientist*. She exects to be able to carry out her research in a free environment with the right to communicate her findings to other scientists. If her research reveals information that is harmful to the economic interests of Green Leaf, she probably expects to report that information as she would any other results.

On the other hand, Dr. Cardoza is also an *employee*. Green Leaf provides her with a place to work, hires assistants for her, provides her with equipment, and pays her a good salary. Doesn't the company have a right to expect loyalty from Dr. Cardoza? Shouldn't she avoid publishing information that will harm the company that employs her?

It's not hard to see how these opposing forces might create a difficult situation for Dr. Cardoza. What if her research at Green Leaf provides even more support for the idea that smoking causes cancer. In an "ideal" setting, Dr. Cardoza's next step would probably be simple and straightforward: write an article about the research, give a speech about her results, or communicate her findings to other scientists in some other way.

But her job at Green Leaf introduces other factors to consider. What does she owe the company for their support of her research? If she knows that her results will bring financial harm to the company, should she withhold those results from her colleagues?

In situations like this, few scientists will lie about their research or will hold back their findings. But they might be willing to qualify their results or to describe their findings in terms that are more favorable to the company's position. Dr. Cardoza might say, for example, that her studies show that more research needs to be done. She might warn against deciding the case of smoking and cancer "too soon" and "before all the evidence is in."

Even scientists who work at universities are not immune from this kind of situation. Many university research projects are financed by companies, associations, federal and state agencies, and other special interest groups. What obligation does a scientist have to the group that pays his or her research bills?

Suppose that the National Association of Coal Mining Companies (NACMC, an imaginary group) funds Dr. Andrew Bascombe's research on industrial fuels. And suppose that Dr. Bascombe finds that some fuel other than coal is a better industrial fuel. Does Dr. Bascombe's report to NACMC complete his *moral* obligations with regard to this research? Or ought he to see to it that other scientists, governmental agencies, and the public at large also hear about his findings?

PUBLIC FUNDING AND PRIVATE PROFIT

The economics of research poses a second ethical dilemma for scientists: who *owns* the ideas that come out of this research? Suppose Dr. Cardoza discovers a method for treating tobacco in such a way as to remove its cancer-causing properties. Is this idea Dr. Cardoza's "property," or does it belong to Green Leaf? Does Dr. Cardoza have the right to advertise, sell, and make a profit on this new procedure? Or should she hand over all rights to the procedure to her employer?

If a scientist works for a private company, the answer

to that question is fairly simple. Most companies ask their employees to sign an agreement which gives to the company all rights for use and sale of any inventions or discoveries the employee makes. This policy makes sense. The company is in business to make money. Part of its money-making plan is to hire people to create ideas and inventions for it. The company pays scientists a good salary in return for this service.

But what if the scientist works for the government or for an academic institution? The new discovery or invention was probably paid for by tax monies in the form of a grant to the scientist. The government is usually not in the business of making and selling new products. In most cases, it probably doesn't want Dr. Cardoza's new idea and might not even know what to do with it if she gave it to the government.

Is it ethical, then, for the scientist to retain control of his or her discovery and to use that discovery to make a personal profit?

The issue of "idea ownership" has received special attention in the area of genetic reseach. Some scientists who had been at the forefront of research in this field formed their own companies in order to market the procedures and products they had developed as a result of their research. The question became, "Is it ethical for a scientist to use knowledge gained at public expense (i.e., tax money) for her or his private profit?"

Some scientists see nothing wrong with using publicly funded discoveries for their own profit. One such scientist has writtten that "The universities are being extremely myopic in trying to create barriers to scientists building commercial enterprises. . . . Given the economic condition of the country and the economic condition of professors, this country is in danger of losing all its good professors to industry."[22]

The fact is that huge amounts of money may be involved in such deals. For example, a University of Cali-

Genetic engineering

fornia professor who founded a biotechnology firm called Genentech, Inc., in 1976, found his stake in the company worth $82 million when it went public four years later. The temptation to cash in on one's research can therefore be very strong.

Not everyone is enthusiastic about this practice, however. Some university officials worry that professors who create private corporations will lose interest in their academic responsibilities. They may concentrate their own university research more on short-term, quick-return projects than on long-term research, which may or may not pay off in the future.

Some scientists also express concern that the practice of scientists' going into business for themselves may corrupt the very nature of science itself. In one instance, a professor established a private company to market some of his research discoveries. That company then offered a grant to the university where the professor worked to pay for more research.

In return for the grant, the professor had agreed *not* to publish his research findings but, instead, to give them directly to the company. Was it ethical for the scientist to carry out his research under these conditions? In this case, his university seemed to think not. It refused to accept the grant because of the conditions to which the professor had agreed.[23]

Neither scientists nor academic institutions have yet agreed on the proper way to deal with this problem. Some universities have taken a practical stand and allowed their professors to create and operate profit-making corporations. Their position seems to be that, ethical or not, the professor's academic contributions are important enough to keep him or her on the staff. Other institutions have decided that it's wrong for scientists to profit from their publicly funded research and have asked scientists to choose between their academic position and potential career with their own for-profit companies.

THE FUNDING OF BASIC RESEARCH

One ethical issue Dr. Cardoza does *not* have to worry about is the relevance of her research. She knows that whatever she finds out about the relationship between smoking and cancer will be of some practical value to someone: the company, smokers, or the general public.

Research designed to solve specific, practical problems is called *applied* research. Efforts to find a cure for cancer, to construct a more efficient jet engine, or to make a better television tube are examples of applied research.

Scientists usually find it relatively easy to obtain money for applied research. When one sets out to solve a practical problem, some business, industry, or government agency is usually willing to supply funds for such research.

But many scientists choose to work on another kind of research. *Basic* (or *pure*) research is motivated solely by an individual's curiosity about a question. Although some practical benefit may result from such research, that is not the reason for which the research is undertaken.

Getting financial support for basic research is usually much more difficult. Who wants to pay for research that may never benefit society? The purpose of the research is simply to learn more about some aspect of nature. Finding out how the universe began, for example, would be an incredibly exciting discovery, but it probably would have not the slightest effect on the daily lives of humans.

Virtually no business, industry, academic institution or private foundation has both the interest in basic research and the money available to support basic research of this scope. So, in practice, basic scientists have really only one source of funding to whom they can turn: the federal government.

The question scientists must consider, then, is wheth-

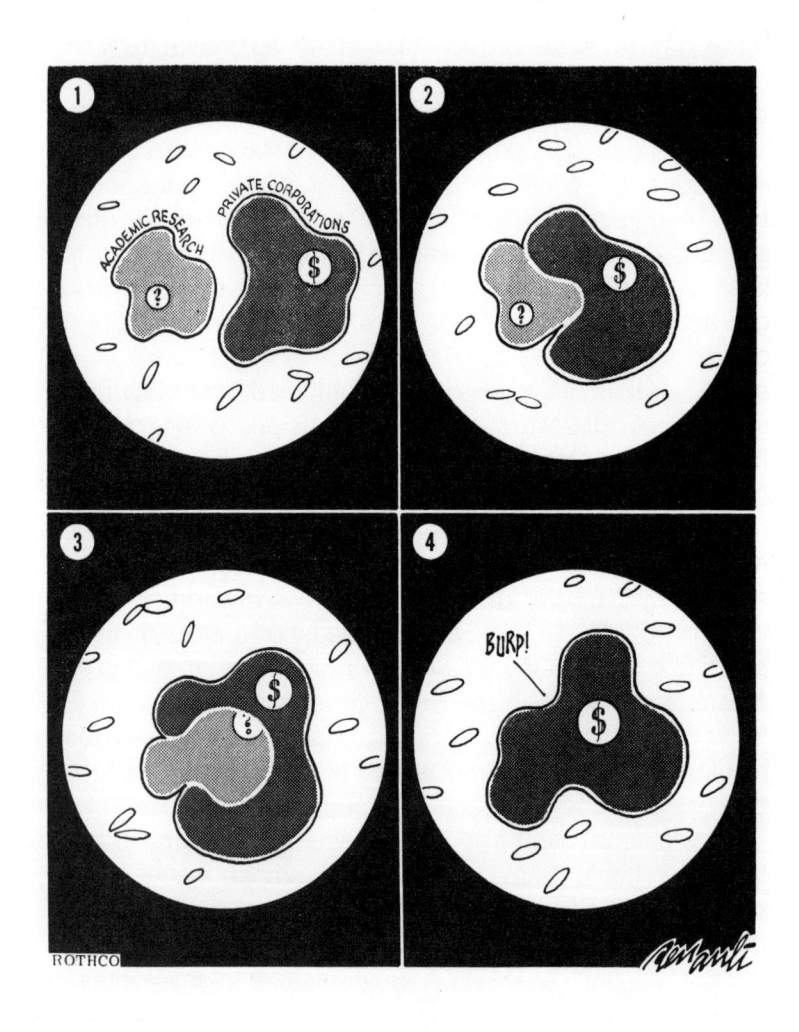

"Fritz has a rather romantic view of science."

er—or to what extent—they should choose a career in basic science. Should a physicist choose basic research on subatomic particles over applied research on energy resources? Should a chemist select basic research on unusual chemical compounds rather than applied research on new building materials?

Those scientists who opt for basic research projects know they are asking for public tax monies to pursue (often very expensive) projects that are primarily of personal interest. They can never *guarantee* that those public dollars will lead to a better life for their fellow citizens. One can argue both sides of this question. First, scientists recognize that progress in science depends absolutely on a solid basis of actual knowledge obtained through basic research. Scientists have a clear professional obligation, therefore, to support and/or carry out basic research.

But simply recognizing that basic research is the cornerstone of scientific progress does not resolve this dilemma. For efforts to connect *particular* examples of basic research with *particular* later inventions and discoveries have not been very successful. And some studies have suggested that no more than 10 percent of all the basic research done ever turns out to have any practical value for society. A scientist may have to ask, then, if he or she is justified in using public monies for *his or her own* particular basic research project.

A more critical question, perhaps, involves the priorities of scientific research. The nation faces many social problems which scientists can help to solve: increasing the food supply, providing better health care, finding new energy sources, and improving systems of transportation, for example.

How important is any basic research project compared to this applied research? Can a scientist really ask for government funds to study the structure of the atom or the origin of the universe knowing that he or she is taking money away from applied research on real social problems?

Some people argue that practical problems such as these will be solved only when scientists have a much better fundamental understanding of the physical world. And that requires basic research. Using public funds for basic research, then, is a completely ethical thing to do.

Other people argue that doing basic research is a prolonged, inefficient, and roundabout way of solving practical problems. To them, it is most ethical to use tax dollars for applied research to solve practical problems now.

Perhaps the most familiar example of this debate in recent years has centered on the U.S. Apollo Project. This program began with President Kennedy's pledge to "put a man on the moon" by the end of the 1960s. The president's promise created an ethical dilemma for scientists and nonscientists alike. The Apollo Program was a large, enormously expensive example of basic research. We could expect to learn a great deal about the earth and the moon from the project.

But the Apollo Project promised no direct, major solutions to the real problems facing humans on earth. At the time of the president's speech, millions of people in the United States and throughout the world were still hungry, in poor health, badly housed, and poorly educated. Could scientists really justify spending billions of tax dollars on a visit to the moon while the immediate personal and social needs of humans were still unsolved?

SECRECY AND CENSORSHIP

A final ethical issue raised by the "Big Business" aspect of science is when, if ever, scientists should withhold information from each other in the interest of security. That issue arises today in two contexts. Consider, first of all, a large biotechnology firm that has just spent five years and a hundred million dollars developing a new product. What freedom would an employee of that company have to disclose information about this product to other scientists?

According to the rules of the game of science, of course, a scientist normally expects to share his or her information with all other interested members of the profession. That simply seems to be the right thing to do for a scientist.

But is it fair to the biotechnology firm, the scientist's employer, for its workers to be telling their colleagues around the world about their research? What will prevent a competitor from picking up valuable information about the new product at a conference, through a journal, or in some other way provided by the "open" communication system in science?

One can imagine how the company could easily lose any head start it might have in such a way. To avoid financial disaster, is the company justified in prohibiting its employees from saying anything about the new product to other scientists?

Ethical questions about the sharing of information have recently become more common also in the field of miltiary research. Today, many scientists in academic institutions finance their research through grants from the Department of Defense (DOD), the National Aeronautics and Space Administration (NASA), and other federal agencies. Everyone knows that a significant portion of this research has potential military applications. Does a scientist working on such a project have the inalienable right to talk about that research in *any* scientific setting whatsoever?

Some government officials have suggested that scientists working in "sensitive" research have a patriotic and moral duty to withhold information under certain circumstances. Do we really want researchers to be talking about ideas that may become parts of new weapons projects at meetings where Russian and Chinese scientists are present, they ask?

One important official at the Department of Defense said in 1985, for example, that "if it was [sic] up to me, I would discourage scientific exchanges between the U.S. and the U.S.S.R."[24]

This policy has, from time to time, prompted the DOD and other government agencies to restrict the flow of information from U.S. scientists. In 1980, for example, the Commerce Department decided that some of the information to be presented at the American Vacuum Society's conference on bubble memory was "sensitive." As a result, scientists from Communist nations were told they could not attend the conference.

In a more recent case, the DOD asked that more than one hundred papers scheduled for presentation at a meeting of the Society of Photo-Optical Instrumentation Engineers be withdrawn. The Department felt that information in these papers could not be released to scientists from other nations.

Overall, eight scientific conferences in 1984 and 1985 were restricted to U.S. citizens because they dealt with "sensitive" topics.[25]

Many—or most—scientists argue the other side of this issue. They say the government has no business interfering with the free flow of information among researchers. The development of science itself has always depended—and continues to depend—on open communication among researchers. Governments will have to find ways other than disrupting this process to protect its military secrets.

Recent legislation has attempted to resolve this conflict. A policy statement signed by President Reagan in October 1985, for example, states that "no restrictions may be placed on the conduct or reporting of federally funded fundamental research that has not received national security classification."[26]

Even when laws, rules (formal and unwritten), customs, and policies exist, they will seldom be the key to finding the "correct" solution to an ethical problem. Instead, each individual scientist will have to weigh factors on both sides of the issue. What does his or her employer have a right to expect from the scientist? What obligations does the scientist have to the profession of science itself? What seems true, honest, and good to the scientist himself or herself in each particular instance? What is best for society?

NOTES

1. *The Encyclopedia Americana* (Danbury, CT: Grolier, Inc, 1986), vol. 14, p. 218.
2. Herta E. Pauli, *Alfred Nobel: Dynamite King—Architect of Peace* (London: Nicholson & Watson, 1947), p. 227.
3. One famous statistician, Sir Ronald Fisher, concluded that Mendel had falsified his data. See Julie Ann Miller, "Mendel's Peas: A Matter of Genius or Guile?" *Science News*, February 18, 1984, p. 108.
4. Miller, p. 109.
5. For more information on this plan, see Stefi Weisburd, "Secrecy and the Seafloor," *Science News*, March 15, 1986, pp. 170-173.
6. The complete story of Alsabti's career is told in William Broad and Nicholas Wade, *Betrayers of the Truth* (New York: Simon and Schuster, 1982), Chapter 3.
7. For a recent retelling of this story, see Michael Bliss, *Banting: A Biography* (Toronto: McClelland and Stewart, 1984).
8. A number of writers have discussed this situation. See, for example, Vern Bullough and Bonnie Bullough, *Sin, Sickness, and Sanity* (New York: New American Library, 1977), Chapter 8; Phyllis Chesler, *Women and Madness* (New York: Doubleday and Company, Inc., 1972); and Carroll Smith-Rosenberg, *Disorderly Conduct* (New York: Oxford University Press, 1985), Part Three.
9. A good discussion of the Burt problem is found in D. D. Dorfman, "The Cyril Burt Question: New Findings," *Science*, September 29, 1978, 1177-1186.
10. For example, a program designed by scientists to inform the public on the value of research with animals is described in Jeffrey L. Fox, "Lab Animal Welfare Issue Gains Momentum," *Science*, February 3, 1984, pp. 468-469.

11. This position is outlined in Thomas H. Moss, "The Modern Politics of Laboratory Animal Use," *Bioscience*, November 1984, pp. 621–625.
12. Keith Schneider, "Weird Science," *Mother Jones*, November/December 1985, p. 45.
13. See Julie Ann Miller, "The Clergy Ponder the New Genetics," *Science News*, March 24, 1984, p. 190.
14. See R. Jeffrey Smith, "Experts Ponder Effect of Pressures on Shuttle Blow-up," *Science*, March 28, 1986, p. 1496.
15. See R. Jeffrey Smith, "Commission Finds Flaw in NASA Decision-making," *Science*, March 14, 1986, p. 1237.
16. Smith, March 28, 1986, p. 1496.
17. Reported in "Launch Critic Punished, Shuttle Panel Told," *San Francisco Examiner and Chronicle*, May 31, 1986, p. 2.
18. For example, see William Shockley, "Dysgenics, Geneticity, Raceology," *Phi Delta Kappan*, January 1972, pp. 297–307; Willaim Shockley, "The Apple-of-God's-Eye Obsession," *The Humanist*, January-February 1972, pp. 16–17; Signe Hammer, "Stalking Intelligence," *Science Digest*, June 1985, p. 37 (sidebar); and note 20, following.
19. See N. L. Gage, "I.Q. Heritability, Race Differences, and Educational Research," *Phi Delta Kappan*, January 1972, pp. 308–312, with response and rejoinder in March 1972, pp. 415–427+. Also see note 20, following.
20. Michael Rogers, "Brave New Shockley," *Esquire*, January 1973, pp. 130+.
21. Guy Wright, "Spying Students," *San Francisco Chronicle*, November 17, 1985, p. A-21.
22. "The Tempest Raging over Profit-minded Professors . . . ," *Business Week*, November 7, 1983, p. 87.
23. *Business Week*, p. 88.
24. *The New York Times*, May 4, 1985, p. 10, as reported in *Current Controversy*, vol. 4, no. 7, 1985, p. 1.
25. For further information, see Irwin Goodwin, "Incident over SPIE Papers Muddies Scientific Secrecy Issue," *Physics Today*, June 1985, pp. 55–57 and Robert L. Park, "Intimidation Leads to Self-censorship in Science," *Bulletin of the Atomic Scientists*, March 1985, pp. 22–25.
26. Irwin Goodwin, "Reagan Issues Order on Science Secrecy: Will It Be Obeyed?" *Physics Today*, November 1985, pp. 55–58. See also Ivars Peterson, "Secrecy, Security and SDI," *Science News*, October 19, 1985, p. 248.

BIBLIOGRAPHY

GENERAL REFERENCES

The Ann Arbor Science for the People Editorial Collective. *Biology as a Social Weapon.* Minneapolis: Burgess, 1977. An outstanding collection of articles showing how unreliable, biased, and fraudulent scientific research can influence social policy.

Bandman, Elsie L., and Bertram Bandman, eds. *Bioethics and Human Rights.* Boston: Little, Brown, 1978. Fifty-three articles dealing with all aspects of bioethical issues.

CHAPTER ONE

Broad, William, and Nicholas Wade. *Betrayers of the Truth.* New York: Simon and Schuster, 1982. The best single reference available on the nature, causes, and effects of fraud in scientific research.

Brody, Howard. *Ethical Decisions in Medicine.* Boston: Little, Brown, 1976. An easy-to-read programmed text dealing with many of the bioethical issues raised in this book.

McCain, Garvin, and Erwin M. Segal. *The Game of Science.* Belmont, Calif.: Brooks/Cole, 1969. An interesting, amusing, and accurate description of the nature of scientific research and the scientific community.

Standen, Anthony. *Science Is a Sacred Cow.* New York: Dutton, 1950. An older, but still excellent book that describes some of the less admirable characteristics of scientists, which you are not likely to read about elsewhere.

CHAPTER TWO

Broad, William, and Nicholas Wade. *Betrayers of the Truth.* New York: Simon and Schuster, 1982.

Sindermann, Carl J. *Winning the Games Scientists Play.* New York: Plenum Press, 1982. A look at some of the things that go on behind the scenes of research in the scientific community.

Weisburd, Stefi. "Secrecy and the Seafloor." *Science News,* March 15, 1986, 170-173.

CHAPTER THREE

Holden, Constance. "A Pivotal Year for Lab Animal Welfare," and Barnes, Deborah M., "Tight Money Squeezes Out Animal Models," *Science,* April 11 and April 18, 1986, 147-150 and 309-311. A series of two articles that review the status of animal experimentation in the United States in the mid-1980s.

Regan, Tom. *The Case for Animal Rights.* Berkeley and Los Angeles: University of California Press, 1983.

Singer, Peter. *Animal Liberation.* New York: Avon Books, 1977.

_____, ed. *In Defense of Animals.* New York: Basil Blackwell, 1985.

CHAPTER FOUR

Baskin, Yvonne. "Doctoring the Genes." *Science 84,* December 1984, 52-60. An excellent discussion of the techniques and some of the ethical issues involved in human gene therapy.

Baum, Rudy M. "Two Critics Look at the Biotechnology Business." *Chemical and Engineering News,* February 3, 1986, 32-33. This review of two new books on ethical issues in biotechnology will give you a quick summary of some of the objections critics are raising about research in genetic engineering.

Biological Sciences Curriculum Study. *Basic Genetics: A Human Approach.* Dubuque, Iowa: Kendall/Hunt Publishing Company, 1983. This book and the three books below present some of the ethical issues involved in genetic, biological, and medical research and applications arising from this research.

_____. *Genes and Surroundings.* Dubuque, Iowa: Kendall/Hunt Publishing Company, 1983.

_____. *Science, Technology, and Society.* Dubuque, Iowa: Kendall/Hunt Publishing Company, 1984.

_____. *Biomedical Technology.* Dubuque, Iowa: Kendall/Hunt Publishing Company, 1984.

Maranto, Gina. "Attack on the Gene Splicers." *Discover,* August 1984, 16-25. A review of some of the social, political, and philosophical (as well as ethical) issues raised by genetic engineering with plants.

Rifkin, Jeremy. *Who Should Play God?* New York: Dell Publishing, 1977. This and the book below contain Rifkin's views on the ethical issues raised by modern scientific research. In connection with the second book, however, be sure also to read the response to these views offered by Stephen Jay Gould in the January 1985 issue of *Discover,* 34-42.

Rifkin, Jeremy, and Nicanor Perlas. *Algeny.* New York: Viking Press, 1983.

Schneider, Keith. "Weird Science." *Mother Jones,* November/December 1985, 40-45. An analysis of Jeremy Rifkin's views on ethical issues in modern scientific research.

CHAPTER FIVE

Ford, Daniel F. *Beyond the Freeze: The Road to Nuclear Sanity.* Boston: Beacon Press, 1982. This book and the two under "Union of Concerned Scientists," below, outline that organization's position on the use of nuclear weapons and the "Star Wars" proposal.

Wilson, Robert R. "The Scientists Who Made the Atom Bomb." *Scientific American,* December 1958. A review of Robert Jungk's *Brighter Than a Thousand Suns: A Personal History of the Atomic Scientists,* one of the best books written about the Manhattan Project.

Yonas, Gerald, and Hans A. Bethe. "Can Star Wars Make Us Safe?" *Science Digest,* September 1985, 30-35+. Opposing viewpoints from two knowledgeable and widely respected scientists.

Union of Concerned Scientists. *The Fallacy of Star Wars.* New York: Vintage Books, 1984. This book and the one below outline the UCS position on the technical, social, economic, political, and ethical issues surrounding the use of nuclear weapons and the "Star Wars" program.

_____. *No First Use.* Cambridge, Mass: The Union of Concerned Scientists, 1983.

CHAPTER SIX

Glazer, Myron. "Ten Whistleblowers and How They Fared." *The Hastings Center Report,* December 1983, 33-41. A summary of the way "whistle-blowing" affected the lives of ten individuals.

CHAPTER SEVEN

Culliton, Barbara J. "Pajaro Dunes: The Search for Consensus." *Science,* April 9, 1982, 155-156+. Report of a conference of academics and industrialists on the problems of their working together on the commercial use of developments in biotechnology.

Goodwin, Irwin. "Reagan Issues Order on Science Secrecy: Will It Be Obeyed?" *Physics Today*, November 1985, 55-58. A good review of the circumstances which lead to the President's actions, with some thoughts about the possible future of federal policy on secrecy in science.

Park, R. L. "Intimidation Leads to Self-Censorship." *Bulletin of the Atomic Scientists*, March 1985, 22-25. The government's recent policies on secrecy in scientific research mean that scientists will operate much more cautiously on their own . . . and that isn't necesarily good.

PERIODICALS AND ORGANIZATIONS

GENERAL PERIODICALS

These often contain articles on ethical issues in science.

American Scientist (New Haven, Conn.)
Audubon (New York)
Bioscience (Washington)
Chemical and Engineering News (Washington)
Discover (Chicago)
Journal of the American Medical Association (Chicago)
Natural History (New York)
Nature (Hampshire, England)
New England Journal of Medicine (Boston)
New Scientist (London)
Physics Today (Easton, Pa.)
Science (Washington)
Science and Government Report (Washington)
Science News (Washington)
Scientific American (New York)

SPECIALIZED PERIODICALS

These focus on ethical issues in science.

Bulletin of the Atomic Scientists (Chicago)
Current Controversy (New York)
Environment (St. Louis)
FAS Newsletter (newsletter of the Federation of American Scientists, Washington)

Impact of Science on Society (Paris)
Issues in Science and Technology (Washington)
PETA News (newsletter of People for Ethical Treatment of Animals, Washington)
Sierra Club Bulletin (San Francisco)
SSRS Newsletter (newsletter of the Society for Social Responsibility in Science, Bala Cynwyd, Pa.)

ORGANIZATIONS

A student organization actively concerned with ethical issues in science is Student Pugwash (USA), 505B Second Street, N.E., Washington, DC, 20002.

INDEX

Academic institutions, 105-106, 108
Action by scientists, 82, 84, 86, 88-90
  choices of, 84
Alsabti, Elias, 38
Altered organisms, 62-67
  opposition to, 66-67
  reasons for, 65-66
Animal experimentation, 49-50, 52, 55-56
Apollo Project, 112
Applied research, 109, 111-112
Archimedes, 74
Arms control, 92-93
Atomic bomb, 74
Attitudes affecting research, 44-47

Basic (pure) research, 109, 111-112
Banting, Dr. Frederick, 42
Best, Dr. Charles, 42
Bulletin of the Atomic Scientists, The, 92-93
Burt, Sir Cyril, 46-47
Business ethics, 81-82
Business profit, 49-50, 52, 55
Business vs. science, 101-102, 104-105, 108-109, 111-115

Cancer, 101-102
Career considerations, 28
Censorship, 112-115
Challenger disaster, 90-92
College degrees, 69
Computer programs, 55-56
Congress, 17

Data, 30, 32-33
  falsifying, 46-47
  "fudging" results of, 33, 35-36
  selection of, 30, 32-33, 35-37
  See also Research
Department of Commerce, 114
Department of Defense, 113-114
Diabetes, 42, 63, 65

Economic factors, 17
E. coli, 62-67
Ethical decisions, 14, 16-17, 19, 47-48, 84, 89-90
  standards for, 19
"Experts," 93, 95-97, 99-100

Falsifying data, 46-47
FDA (Food and Drug Administration), 17
First Amendment rights, 95

Fraud in science, 35-36
"Fudging" results, 33, 35-36
Funding, 109, 111-112

Genentech, Inc., 108
Genetic engineering, 63, 65, 68-71
Genetic research, 62-71, 106, 108
Genetics, 30
Germ cells, 70
Graduate students, 40, 42
Grants, 27-28, 30

Heredity vs. environment, 46-47
Human gene therapy (HGT), 68, 70-71
Human growth hormone (HGH), 70-71
Humans for experimentation, 50, 56-61
　arguments against, 58-61
　informed consent in, 58

Ideas, 105-106, 108
　acknowledging sources of, 38-39
　See also Plagiarism
Informed consent, 58
Insulin, 42

Kennedy, President John F., 112

Laboratory animals, 50, 52, 55-56
Legal factors, 17
Lesch-Nyhan disease, 68, 70-71

Macleod, Dr. John J. R., 42
Massachusetts Institute of Technology (MIT), 92
Mendel, Gregor, 30-32
Military research, 72-80
Moral considerations, 113
Morton Thiokol, 90-92

National Aeronautics and Space Administration (NASA), 113
National Oceanic and Atmospheric Administration, 36-37
National security, 36-37

Navy, U.S., 36
Newton, Sir Isaac, 37
Nobel, Alfred, 21-23
Nobel Prize, 23, 39, 42, 97
Nuclear power plants, 92-93

Objectivity. See Scientific objectivity
Ocean floor mapping, 36-37
O-ring gaskets, 90-92

Patriotic considerations, 77, 79
Patriotic duty, 113
Permission for experimentation, 60
Philosophical considerations, 67
Physicians' responsibilities, 61
Plagiarism, 37, 39
　and graduate students, 40, 42
Presidential Commission, 90-92
Professors, 106, 108
Profit, 105-106, 108
Public funding, 105-106, 108
Public safety, 62-67
Publishing research, 106, 108

Reagan, President Ronald, 99, 114
Religious considerations, 17
Religious objections, 70
Research, 49-61
　on animals, 49-50, 52, 55-56
　applied, 109, 111-112
　attitudes affecting, 44-47
　basic, 109, 111-112
　computers in, 55-56
　credit for, 37-39
　funding of, 109, 111-112
　on humans, 50, 56-61
　publishing of, 106, 108
Rifkin, Jeremy, 67, 70-71

Science and business, 101-115
Scientific method, 20
Scientific objectivity, 44-47
Scientific research, 27-48
　See also Research
Scientists, 24, 26
　as employees, 104-105
　ethical decisions of, 21, 23-24, 26

Scientists
(continued)
   as "experts," 93, 95-97, 99-100
   opinions of, 96, 99-100
   as protestors, 87-100
   and Vietnam War, 92
Secrecy, 112-115
"Sensitive" topics, 114
Shockley, Dr. William B., 97, 99
Smoking and cancer, 101-102
Snow, C.P., 96
Social action groups, 92-93
Society of Photo-Optical Instrumentation Engineers, 114
Space-based weapons systems, 92-93
"Star Wars"
   See Strategic Defense Initiative (SDI)
Strategic Army Defense System (SADS), 72-73
Strategic Defense Initiative (SDI), 80, 92-93, 99
Subjectivity in research, 44-47

"Top secret" classification, 24

Union of Concerned Scientists (UCS), 92-93
Union of Soviet Socialist Republics (USSR), 113-114
U.S. Navy, 36
University of California, 106, 108
Use of others' work, 37-40, 42.
   See also Plagiarism
Usselman, Dr. Mel, 32-33

Vietnam War, 92, 96
Volunteers, 58, 60

Waste disposal sites, 62-67
Weapons development, 92-93
Weapons research, 73, 77, 79-80
   arguments against, 79-80
   arguments for, 77, 79
   ethical considerations, 80
"Whistle-blowers," 89
Women, 45-46, 48
Wright, Guy, 99

ABOUT THE AUTHOR

David E. Newton has taught science and mathematics at nearly every grade level, from elementary through postgraduate. He was formerly professor of chemistry at Salem State College and visiting professor of science education at Western Washington University. He is currently adjunct professor in the College of Professional Studies at the University of San Francisco, where he teaches a course in science and social issues. Dr. Newton is the author of thirty-one books and over three hundred other publications.